HOW
TO
PASS
LAW
EXAMS

HOW TO PASS LAW EXAMS

PETER D FRASER

Illustrated by Graham Sedgwick

HLT Publications

HLT PUBLICATIONS

200 Greyhound Road, London W14 9RY

First published 1991
Reprinted 1992
© The HLT Group Ltd 1991

ISBN 0 7510 0001 9

British Library Cataloguing-in-Publication

A CIP Catalogue record for this book
is available from the British Library

Printed and bound in Great Britain

CONTENTS

Foreword by Dr P.A. Linehan

1 INTRODUCTION   1

2 PLANNING YOUR REVISION   7

3 NOTES   25

4 CASES AND STATUTES   39

5 THE EXAMS THEMSELVES   55

6 ESSAY AND PROBLEM TYPE QUESTIONS   73

7 FINE TUNING   89

8 DOING IT IN STYLE   103

FOREWORD

From the allegedly innovative nature of the system expounded in the following pages there is much to be learned about the thought processes of those to whom the administration of justice in this country will one day be entrusted.

Not often does a person of Peter Fraser's qualities come a tutor's way. This is one of the proofs for the existence of God. As PDF's former minder during his period of shore-leave by the Cam, I am less surprised that he should have written this book than dismayed that his central nervous system has degenerated to such an extent that he judges it advantageous to associate me with his scheme of foisting it upon an unsuspecting public.

A puce-faced lad of some twenty summers, incapable of telling a tort from a rowlock, in 1983 PDF embarked upon what by his lights was a brilliant career. Within every Adrian Mole there is a C.B. Fry trying to get out. And the justly underrated Peter certainly tried (Peter *always* tried). But somehow the Adrian in him always prevailed. A shy boy, always with nicely polished shoes and ink pen tucked under his college scarf, to those of us who valued ordinariness Peter appeared a deeply reassuring figure. How wrong we were. Only now, in reading this brave and in its way moving testimony, are we able to appreciate the turmoil of this tortured soul: the xenophobia; the bulimia (croissants all morning *and* lunch with his too indulgent tutor); the obsession with Corinthian computer scientists. The fantasising about foreign parts experienced Fraser-watchers were already familiar with: his section on Holidays will be regarded as authoritative. But so no doubt will all of *How To Pass Law Exams*. The work of a writer of culture as wide as he is deep, this classic of its kind invites comparison with *Old Moore's Almanack* and *Whiffle on the Care of the Pig*. No provincial bedsit, however grotty, will be able to deny it a place on its bookshelf, and the prospect of a sequel, which its author threatens, suggests that it may even be taken down occasionally and read with the care and attention it deserves.

Peter Linehan
July 1991

1
INTRODUCTION

If you are supremely confident about your exams, without a doubt in your mind that you are going to pass with flying colours, then this book can only amuse you as you realise quite how much the mere mortals have to do. If you *are* so confident, you must have copious amounts of beautifully kept notes. That enormous lever-arch file, so heavy it takes three strong men to lift it – oh, how you are envied. Throughout this book, you, the male and female of the lever-arch species, will be called Cyril and Shirley.

However, if you are one of those (not quite so dull) people who actually missed a few lectures, was struck down with some mystery illness and so missed a tutorial or two, or had a succession of excellent excuses for missing all those Land Law supervisions (namely that they prejudiced your good health and sanity), then despair not. All those guilty afternoons can be redeemed.

You *can* pass the exams.

There *is* enough time.

You *will* get some notes.

And, best of all, there is a very good chance that you will achieve as good a pass as Cyril and Shirley with the groaning lever-arch file. There are three ways to go about this, only one of which is recommended.

a) Break into the Faculty and steal the exam papers. Then bribe a Research Student to prepare model solutions (pay no more than two pints of scrumpy or offer to trim his (or her) beard for free), and learn the answers by heart.

b) Cosh either Cyril or Shirley (or both of them, if you're feeling light-hearted) over the head, and steal the lever-arch file. A degree of dramatic irony can be achieved by coshing them *with* the lever-arch file, before stealing it. Then learn the entire contents, whilst in Wormwood Scrubs awaiting trial. You will not, however, be permitted to take your exams by correspondence course.

c) Folllow this book. You're already way ahead of the game by having bought it in the first place. And if you *haven't* bought it, and are reading a friend's copy, then *PUT IT DOWN AT ONCE!* How dare you abuse your position of trust by sneaking a look in this valuable work? You'll never make a success of it in the law with that sort of attitude. Change subjects to computer studies at once.

You will now have realised that (c) above is the best way to approach the task. Besides, prisons are cramped and unfriendly places.

The reason that a method such as this one can actually work is a simple one. The vast majority of your talents are never even used, and never will be used. I am just going to help you use a little more than you're used to, that's all.

Also, and on this one I am perfectly prepared to be proved wrong by you, you probably work (if you work at all), in an appallingly disorganised and inefficient way. Once you get into the big, bad world, and have to actually work for a living, you will realise just how much time you have on your hands and how little you accomplish in that time.

Imagine for a moment that you have a job. (Shock, horror! I know, it's dreadful. But use your imagination, just for a moment.) At the very least, you will have to work for about 40 hours a week. That means Monday to Friday, 9.00 in the morning (or thereabouts) until 5.30 each evening. And that's only if you have a non-stressed, ordinary sort of life. If you are an eager beaver and/or intent on working hard and/or desperate to make lots of loot, you may very well find yourself working a lot harder and longer than that. Even at weekends in extreme cases! (For those of you who get too depressed when thinking about such things, take heart and look on the bright side of life. It could be worse. You could be a medic, facing 120-hour weeks, every other weekend, no pay to speak of and exams until you're 30 years old. Be of good cheer – and try to stay in good health.)

Now, contrast that with your present life-style. How many hours' work did you do last week? (I'll let you off if it was a week's vacation.) One? Two? You will be a very unusual student if you spent more than ten hours working. In fact, if you spent as many as ten hours working (and no, of course you don't count hours spent in tutorials) give yourself a large pat on the back. For the other 99.9 per cent of my thousands of readers, who spent more time in the local hostelry or playing dungeons and dragons (only kidding – the booksellers have instructions not to sell this to people who look as if they play dungeons and dragons) ... shame on you!

And yet, if you look at the broader picture, even if you did work as many as ten hours in a week it wouldn't exactly ruin your carefree life, would it? I think you could fit in 10 am until noon each morning, don't you? Just on Monday to Friday; you can still have the weekend off if you like. It would not be too dreadful – you can still spend countless hours fishing, drinking and engaging in athletic pursuits of one sort or another if you want.

All you have to do is actually get out of bed by 9 or 9.30 am. And don't use that feeble excuse that you would miss lectures – you probably miss lectures anyway, for nowhere near as good a reason as being in the library working.

So you had better start mending your ways, you lazy good-for-nothing apology for a scholar. If you're lucky enough to be reading this near to the start of the academic year, then buckle down and you will have so much less to do once exam panic comes around at Easter time.

However, you may not be lucky enough to be preparing your assault on the bastions of the faculty as early as October or November. It may already be Easter. The daffodils may be in bloom, the Boat Race may have come and gone and you may have no chance to redeem your worthless existence other than this excellent ten-week plan which I am generous enough to share with you.

However, there will doubtless be sceptics amongst you who think that ten weeks is far too little time to redeem your hopeless situation, that you are going to fail and nothing can be done about it.

The first response to that pathetic argument is, if it is certain that you *will* fail, you have nothing to lose by trying, have you? All you will have missed out on is ten weeks doing nothing, and if you do fail you will have plenty more opportunity to do nothing as you wait for those job offers that never come. (Quite a philosophical and logical riposte, I think.)

The second response is: what makes you so sure you *cannot* make it in ten weeks? Mankind has put men on the moon. Hannibal took all those elephants across the Alps (I'm no student of history but I bet that didn't take much longer than ten weeks). Carthorses have won the Grand National. Miracles *do* happen. You may as well try, because you certainly have nothing whatsoever to lose. Prove your critics (and that may well include your tutor) wrong.

So, assuming that you *do* want to go on, there are several preliminary steps that you have to take, in addition of course to the pledge that you will follow this book faithfully.

You must steel yourself for the arduous task ahead. You must forego those binges when you consume so much alcohol that the following day you cannot remember even your name, let alone the jurisprudential justification for the doctrine of assumpsit. You must, for ten short weeks, assume the lifestyle and approach of a true academic. Yes, that means you will have to go to the library. Who knows, you may even enjoy it!

Whether you enjoy it or not, at least you will have had a go. And as they used to say in the Flashing Blade, it is better to have fought and lost, than not to have fought at all. So come on – put down that bagel with cream cheese! To arms!

So, on to Chapter 2 and the beginning of the real work. Up until now, we've just been chewing the ... what is the American expression? I've never really understood it anyway. Gird your loins! Prepare for the fray! The next ten weeks will be the most ... interesting so far. Perhaps 'interesting' is the wrong word, but here we go anyway.

2
PLANNING YOUR REVISION

The linch-pin of the whole plan is the 'six Ps', a tried and trusted motto that lead to the introduction of my system. Used by everyone from NASA astronauts to eager students like you, like most excellent things it is very simple:

Proper Planning and Preparation Prevents

Poor Performance

Though the expression of the motto would doubtless be obvious to most people, in the heat of the exam season it is often forgotten that a little time and planning used to organise everything can yield great dividends. In my opinion this motto sums up beautifully the need for a clear and full plan that is going to help you achieve your 'academic peak' about 2–3 hours before your first exam. Do not worry should this be a morning exam. You will not necessarily need to get up at 6 am to peak properly before your first paper.

In order to prepare a plan in detail, I am going to have to make certain assumptions regarding what subjects you are taking. After detailed market research, it has been discovered that most of the readers of this aid to scholarship will be law students. Bearing in mind the title, that is not too surprising, you might feel. Anyway, so that the most help can be given to the most people, I am going to draw up a sample plan for a notional eager bright-eyed young Corinthian who is taking five papers, those being Land Law, Equity and Trusts, Law of the European Community, Sale of Goods and Consumer Credit (all one paper) and Family Law. I have chosen this wholly arbitrary selection because it includes:

a)   two subjects, Land Law and Equity and Trusts that are compulsory and part of the six so-called 'core' subjects for those who wish to practise either at the Bar or as solicitors;

b)   one paper that is, for revision purposes, two different subjects with a broad connection, Sale of Goods and Consumer Credit. Often option papers will include two subjects in this way.

Most universities and polytechnics that use the yearly (or 'tripos') system require five papers to be taken in a single academic year. Those attending institutions that still cling to the unhelpful notion whereby *all* the subjects studied throughout the course are examined in the final term will almost certainly have more than five papers to take in one go. If you are one of these unfortunates you will have to adapt the concept to take account of the 6–7 extra papers for which you need to revise.

The first thing that you must do to help draw up the plan is to list all the *topic* headings of each paper. I must emphasise here that the following headings are only of an *illustrative* nature. If you happen to be taking one of the papers that I have listed in my group of five, do *not* take the topic lists as an exhaustive list of those you need to cover in your own revision. Your syllabus may be different from mine – seeing as I drew mine up on the back of a cereal packet over breakfast, I *hope* your syllabus is different – and you will inevitably be more up-to-date than me. After all, you read *all* the law reports in the broadsheets, don't you? Of course you do, and jolly interesting they are too!

The following topics need to be incorporated into the programme. The topics appear below the name of the paper in the following table.

LAND LAW	EQUITY AND TRUSTS	LAW OF THE EC	SALE OF GOODS AND CREDIT	FAMILY LAW
Registered land	Maxims of equity	Directives	Sale of goods	Marriage
Unregistered land	Express trusts	Judgments	Property and risk	Divorce
LPA 1925 reforms	Resulting trusts	The European Court	The 1979 Act	Child protection
Leases	Charitable trusts	Direct effect	ss14–17	Domestic violence
Trusts for sale	Constructive trusts	Direct applicability	s18 – the 5 rules	*Caunce* v *Caunce*
Co-ownership	Trustees	Taxes and duty	nemo dat quod non habet	Matrimonial home protection
Fixtures	Breach of trust	Free trade	Debtor-creditor-supplier agreements	*S* v *S*; *M* v *M*; *A* v *A*
Restrictive covenants	Equitable remedies	Protection of rights	CC Act 1974	Adoption
Clogs and fetters and other Dutch variants	Tracing	*Cassis de Dijon*	Revolving credit	Juveniles
Mortgages	Administration	*Wensch*	Formalities	Wills

The next thing to do is draw up a simple calendar of each week between today's date and the end of the exams. This obviously must include each individual day, and Saturdays and Sundays too. Do not make the mistake of ignoring the potentially 'spare' days between exams themselves – you may even be lucky enough to have a week's gap before your last paper, for example.

If this is the case, then give careful consideration to leaving most of your revison work for that paper until after the first four papers are over. It is much easier to do well, the fewer papers for which you have to study; this is somewhat obvious. By leaving the bulk of one paper until the others are over, you will be acting as though you are only taking four papers, not five.

A note of caution, however. This is only feasible when there is an *appreciable* gap; in my opinion, there must be at least five clear days between the fourth paper and the fifth. Also, if there is even the smallest chance that after your four papers are over you will get 'demob happy' and take it easy, then forget it.

You must realise that it is essential that you keep your nerve, motivation and discipline for the whole programme, and that means until you are leaving the exam hall after answering *all* the necessary questions in your *final* paper. After that, you can do whatever you like, and I hope that includes as many strange and bizarre practices as you are able to think up. However, *until* then, you must not waver. It's not over until it's over, as the West Indian fast-bowler said having been called for a no-ball. Let me give you an example.

(For this example we will assume that the aim here is merely to pass.) Suppose you have done your first four papers. They have gone relatively well and so you feel that the pressure is off completely, and that all you have to do is have a go at the last paper. You feel that you have done most, if not all, of the real work.

This is *absolutely wrong*, and by thinking in such a way you risk ruining all the other good work that you've already done. Even on a very simplistic view of marking, your final paper will count for a maximum of 20 per cent of your overall mark. That potential mark can of course make the difference between passing and failing. Furthermore, the Faculty may adopt the method whereby each paper is given a 'class' (such as First, Upper Second, Lower Second, Third etc) and then an overall class is awarded. In such a case, a poor fifth result like a Third or even a Fail can have a disproportionate effect on the result as a whole. It may even cause you to fail altogether. The law of diminishing returns, which we will cover in detail when talking about exam essay questions, does not apply when you are taking five different papers.

So this timetable assumes:

a) there are ten weeks to the exams, which are to be taken on the days shown, starting at the beginning of April;

b) there are no helpful gaps of five clear days or more as already discussed;

c) the number of days off to be taken starts with one and a half days a week, and reduces to only half a day just before the exams;

d) we change up a gear in earnest with two weeks to go.

Example Timetable for the Ten Week Plan

Week 1	Day 1	Wed	Land
(break you in	Day 2	Thurs	Land
gently – just a	Day 3	Fri	Land
three-day week)	Day 4	Sat	Off
	Day 5	Sun	Off
Week 2	Day 6	Mon	Trusts
	Day 7	Tues	Trusts
	Day 8	Wed	Trusts
	Day 9	Thurs	EC
	Day 10	Fri	EC
	Day 11	Sat	am: EC
	Day 12	Sun	Off
Week 3	Day 13	Mon	SGA/CC
	Day 14	Tues	SGA/CC
	Day 15	Wed	SGA/CC
	Day 16	Thurs	Family
	Day 17	Fri	Family
	Day 18	Sat	am: Family
	Day 19	Sun	Off
Week 4	Day 20	Mon	Land
	Day 21	Tues	Land
	Day 22	Wed	Trusts
	Day 23	Thurs	Trusts
	Day 24	Fri	EC
	Day 25	Sat	EC
	Day 26	Sun	Off

Week 5	Day 27	Mon	SGA/CC
	Day 28	Tues	SGA/CC
	Day 29	Wed	Family
	Day 30	Thurs	Family
	Day 31	Fri	Family
	Day 32	Sat	EC
	Day 33	Sun	Off
Week 6	Day 34	Mon	EC
	Day 35	Tues	Land
	Day 36	Wed	Land
	Day 37	Thurs	Land
	Day 38	Fri	Trusts
	Day 39	Sat	am: Trusts
	Day 40	Sun	Off
Week 7	Day 41	Mon	Trusts
	Day 42	Tues	EC
	Day 43	Wed	EC
	Day 44	Thurs	Family
	Day 45	Fri	Land
	Day 46	Sat	am: Family
	Day 47	Sun	EC
Week 8	Day 48	Mon	EC
	Day 49	Tues	Family
	Day 50	Wed	Family
	Day 51	Thurs	SGA/CC
	Day 52	Fri	SGA/CC
	Day 53	Sat	Land
	Day 54	Sun	Off

Week 9	Day 55	Mon	Trusts
	Day 56	Tues	Trusts
	Day 57	Wed	EC
	Day 58	Thurs	EC
	Day 59	Fri	Family
	Day 60	Sat	Family
	Day 61	Sun	am: SGA/CC
Week 10	Day 62	Mon	EC
	Day 63	Tues	Trusts
	Day 64	Wed	Trusts
	Day 65	Thurs	Family
	Day 66	Fri	SGA/CC
	Day 67	Sat	Off
	Day 68	Sun	Land
	(68 days of work – incredible!)		
Week 11	Day 69	Mon	Land Exam
(Exams)	Day 70	Tues	Trusts Exam
	Day 71	Wed	EC Exam
	Day 72	Thurs	SGA/CC
	Day 73	Fri	SGA/CC Exam
	Day 74	Sat	Off
.	Day 75	Sun	Family
Week 12	Day 76	Mon	Family Exam
(Exams)	Day 77	Tues	Party!
	Day 78	Wed	Headache

In my opinion, it is really only a matter of common sense. However, common sense is, like an English fast-bowler, a precious and rare commodity.

Make the necessary adjustments to the timetable depending on exactly when the exams fall, and then each day all that is required is a quick look at the timetable and you will know exactly what subject you have to work on that day.

The fundamental principles of the plan are as follows:

a)   ensure that a subject is revised the day immediately *before* that exam;

b)   weight the timetable (if necessary) *towards* those subjects that you do not like, and that you are no good at (or should I say *less* good at, since I'm being paid to give you spirit and fortitude);

c)   always have *at least* half a day off per week as a minimum, and until the last couple of mad weeks try to have a full day off each week;

d)   keep the duration of any one subject-block relatively short. This makes it easier to stay interested (apologies if I'm under-estimating your powers in this regard). As you can see from the above timetable, no single block is any longer than three or four days and this happens more in the earlier stages of the timetable (the reason for this will become more clear in the chapter on Notes);

e)   and of course the golden rule is to adhere rigidly to the timetable.

Now sticking to the timetable, you have a structure within which to work. There is no need to concern your mind with the dull detail of what to study and when. This way you are not taking up valuable brain capacity thinking about irrelevant details like whether to pick up your file on Roman Law or the one on Equity. (Scholars have a difficult choice in such situations – the rest of you probably pick up the morning paper.)

The most important thing to do is be honest with yourself with regard to how much you are actually doing each day and how much you have to do. If you have decided, for example, to work between the hours of 9 am and 12.30 pm for your 'morning' sessions, then don't read the newspaper until 9.20 and fool yourself that you're working because you glance at the law report (if the paper you're reading actually *has* a law report, that is).

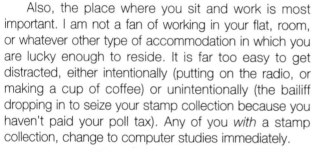

Also, the place where you sit and work is most important. I am not a fan of working in your flat, room, or whatever other type of accommodation in which you are lucky enough to reside. It is far too easy to get distracted, either intentionally (putting on the radio, or making a cup of coffee) or unintentionally (the bailiff dropping in to seize your stamp collection because you haven't paid your poll tax). Any of you *with* a stamp collection, change to computer studies immediately.

Furthermore, the demarcation line between work and time-off is not sufficiently clear-cut if you work at home. Working at home is a nightmare fraught with difficulties and is to be avoided if at all possible. Obviously if you are a so-called 'mature' student (an oxymoron if ever I wrote one) and caring for two young children then it's a different matter. You will of course have to take the kids to the left-luggage facility at the nearest railway station each morning. (If I were you I'd leave them at the left-luggage for the whole ten weeks anyway. Who can afford a crèche?)

So you must choose a place to work for the whole of your ten-week period. Ideally this would be a library. The advantages of a library are numerous. There is usually a rule of silence that certainly should discourage the weak from chatting and otherwise wasting valuable time. (Yes, by 'weak' I mean *YOU*.) The presence of other hard-working scholars will, hopefully, encourage you and may even inspire you! Because the library will, at the least, be a short walk from where you live (for those lucky few) and more probably a heck of a hike (for the vast majority, especially those in London and other cities), you will have some advantages, such as:

a) having less incentive to nip home for a cup of tea and to watch the lunchtime news and/or an Australian soap opera on television;

b) a clear demarcation line existing between the library (dreadfully dull but you know you have to do it) and home (where you can relax without worrying about reading your notes etc);

c) a consequentially early start into the type of life you will have when you start working. This is at best a mixed blessing, but at least it can help to point out to you just how easy life is whilst studying.

But there are disadvantages too. Firstly, you will have to find out where the library is – after all, you have avoided doing so thus far in your slightly murky academic career. For those of you who find this investigative task beyond you – you guessed it. Computer studies for you! Next, you may have to convince the librarian (or any other factotum whose job is to be unpleasant to users of the library as they are an unwelcome interruption) that you are a bona fide student, as they will not recognise your finely chiselled features.

But, most difficult of all, you will have to find a *seat* in the library. This can be very tricky indeed, as you will find to your infinite amusement. There are two approaches to this.

a) Try to be diplomatic about it without alienating those who have been in the library for the last few months.

b) Deliberately alienate all those who have been in the library for the last few months. I find that sitting on someone's lap until they move and surrender their seat quite effective, particularly if you then repeat the process elsewhere once you find you cannot stare out of the window from the seat that you have initially chosen.

Either way you establish your own seat and are ready to begin. Incidentally, if in the weeks to come someone sits in *your* seat, you deal with it by pretending they're not there and, again, sitting on top of them until they move. Very effective, particularly if you have a very bony bottom.

METHOD OF WORKING

First of all, you must disabuse yourself of any notion you may have that this is going to be easy. True, you have a head start, having the guidance of a work such as this – pitfalls may await you, but any pitfall can be successfully navigated with help. But if you think that this means passing will be a stroll, then think again. Prepare yourself mentally for the worst, then the reality will be a pleasant surprise. Because in the same way that First Division teams get knocked out by non-league minnows in the Cup, if you take it easy the examiner will knock *you* out, and take great pleasure in doing it.

Secondly, great plans need to be prepared, but you must *stick* to the plans. It is no good going to great lengths (as we shall) to plan this coup, only to pay more attention to the *Racing News* than your timetable. You have had your fun and games – now, this is a serious business and it's head down and nose to the grindstone until the last exam is over. I hate to sound like either Cyril or Shirley, but think how much greater your relief will be if you actually get your act together (for once) and do well. It's only for ten weeks, after all!

Thirdly, our scheme is a tried-and-tested one and you must have no truck with the absurd posturing of the midnight oil brigade. By that I do not mean that you are not permitted to listen to tracks by that excellent Australian band, Midnight Oil. Oh no. What I mean is you will doubtless be aware of that brand of fool who sits in the library until 3 am, is kicked out by the porter and then reads his notes in bed until 5 am. He will appear from time to time, looking like death on a good day, and then disappear back into his nocturnal world. If that is how you want to play it, then fine, but start looking *now* through the Sits Vac columns for a job for after you've failed the exams.

So, now we've got all those little misconceptions out of the way, a brief word about the style of working you should adopt. All of this procedure assumes that you have been smart enough to buy this book sufficiently in advance of the exams to give yourself at least ten weeks.

If you have less than that, or cannot be dissuaded from taking that three-week trip to the Caribbean just before the exams, then obviously you will have to adapt the programme somewhat. (You will have an advantage, however, when we get to the chapter on 'Doing it in Style'.)

Each day is split up into morning, afternoon and evening sessions. Until two or three weeks before Day 1 (ie the day of your first exam) I do not recommend that you work for more than two of each of these daily sessions. Personally, I used to work morning and afternoon, because I always have evening plans (more of which later). Also, the exams are usually at these times of day, and I think it worthwhile to get used to working at the time of day that you will be put through the hoop at the Faculty.

It does not really matter which of these sessions you choose to work in; however, you must keep to the same ones each day. The important thing is to get into a *routine*. We will discuss this in greater depth later, but you have to get your worthless carcass into the habit of set times for work. You will find that a framework helps you to get through those dreadful, long hours when you sit there staring out of the window, hoping for inspiration. (It will rarely come, but don't worry about that yet; you'll only get depressed.)

However, you must not fool yourself, as I said. My tutor had an excellent technique of inviting some of us to lunch about a week or two before the exams. There were always those who didn't feel they could attend – pressure of work, you know – and you can imagine how much *those* fun party animals were missed. Those of us who actually did drag ourselves away from the delights of the Sale of Goods Act (yes, we were studying Family Law and reading around our subject) had a truly relaxing and enjoyable day. We would then return to the fray refreshed and ready to absorb even more excitement. But you cannot get the benefit of such treats unless you put the really hard work in first.

Combined and 'Half' Papers

One example of combined papers is the one above, namely Sale of Goods and Consumer Credit. Usually such combined papers will consist of two subjects that have a general connection, such as in this example. Rather obvious really – that is why they are combined. To approach this correctly you need to know the rules regarding the paper. How is it set out? Is it split into two distinct sections, with the examinee having to answer at least two questions from each? If so, then you will need to be as switched-on and up-to-date on each of the two subjects, because in reality it will be like taking two different subjects. A poor performance in Sale of Goods, for example, could cost you the entire paper.

Rather obvious again, you may think. But it is worth looking up the regulations on this point. There may be a requirement only that you answer a minimum of one question for each of the two sections, and you can answer the remaining questions (probably another two or three) from whichever section you like. In such circumstances, it may be worth your while concentrating all your efforts on one of the two subjects. Obviously this will depend on your aptitude in each of the two on offer.

For example, there are many people who find the concept (if there is such a thing) behind Sale of Goods quite unfathomable. You may be one of them. Furthermore, because you are such a wild-eyed bohemian, you do not find this out until April (by which time it is too late to change subjects) because you do no work until April. Try as you might, you cannot get to grips with the different ideas of property, passing of risk and the other madcap ideas very easily or at all. On the other hand, consumer credit is much more straightforward. You bought your CD player on HP and were really interested in the exciting agreement that came with details of your monthly payments. So, you concentrate on Consumer Credit and learn only enough Sale of Goods to get through one, most obvious, question. (A side benefit of this is that you realise you entered into an 'extortionate credit bargain' when you bought the CD player and so you apply to the Court to be released therefrom. Law does have some uses, after all.)

There are dangers in this approach. You must know your specialist subject *very well indeed*. In an exam where you are required to answer five questions altogether, you will have to answer four on Consumer Credit. Also, you cannot totally ignore the booby subject either, in this case Sale of Goods. You have to be able to answer that one question, the *obvious* one (see Question Spotting later) well enough so that it doesn't let you down. But this technique can work very well indeed, and may be worth considering.

'Half' papers are a different matter entirely. These are papers two of which make up a full paper, but they are all self-contained and have little or no relation to other subjects. The idea behind them is to give those of you with a real taste for the subject (like Intellectual Property or Landlord and Tenant) the opportunity to sample different fields. My opinion is, avoid them. The amount of work required to do a half paper well is probably more than you are planning on doing for any of your full papers. But I do know at least one very unintelligent person who pulled off something of a coup by choosing half papers, so I may be wrong. The adage 'half a paper for half a candidate' may have some truth in it after all.

Once the dreadful days are upon you and it is less than two weeks to the exams, then the scenario changes and you change up a gear. This is dealt with more fully later – and no skipping ahead to see how it is done. All in good time will the secrets be revealed.

I must emphasise that you *should* take a day off when one is programmed. I will certainly not be impressed with your working ten weeks without a day off, and you won't be impressed when you fail your exams because you're jaded. If you subscribe to the flair school of study, the last insult anyone should be able to fling at you is that you're jaded. Laid-back, yes. Cutting it fine, perhaps. Jaded, *never*.

Have some style – who wants to end up like Cyril and Shirley? Even if you don't take all the style hints in the chapter on 'Doing It in Style' (remember, no skipping ahead!), try not to be a nerd *deliberately*. Even Cyril and Shirley have an excuse – they don't know any better. You *do*, however, and if, sadly, you both lack the pazzazz *and* are indisputably dull enough to turn down a day off, then I am appalled that my work is being put to such use. Two questions: have you ever thought of switching to computer studies, and are you called either Cyril or Shirley?

Finally, take each chapter in turn. The only exception to this is, in exceptional circumstances, 'Doing It in Style'. However, if you actually *need* to be told how to do it in style, then perhaps it would be rash of you to take that chapter out of turn and risk spoiling the effect.

So on to Chapter 3 and the beginning of the real work. Up until now, we've just been setting the scene. This is what the chorus would have done in a Shakespearian play, before quaffing flagons of mead. But no mead for you yet. Now you are ready for the next demanding stage. You need to acquire some notes. You are ready to do battle. Sally forth into the next chapter secure in the knowledge that, thus far, you are doing fine.

3
NOTES

This is one of the areas where Cyril and Shirley are obviously way ahead of you at the moment. Doubtless all those mornings spent lying in bed, or working out, when you should have been at lectures, were the most tremendous fun. However, you missed out on that essential area: note creation. Note creation is most important, and there are several reasons for this. Most people find it difficult, not to say impossible, to revise from textbooks. I dare say some of you reading this find it difficult, not to say impossible, to revise at all. It is the one area where schooldays were so effortlessly easy, because the whole process of lessons, exercise books and homework created for you a set of notes which you could use come the exams.

Of course, at the time you didn't realise quite how lucky you were – after all, you had never been in the situation where you had taken nearly an entire academic year and done practically nothing at all! And besides, whilst you were at school, sitting at your desk writing reams about Jane Austen's satire of the Gothic Novel, the last thing on your mind was: 'Oh, how lucky I am having all this dictated to me by Miss Brodie; I will have such good notes for my forthcoming exam.' More likely you were wondering how you could manage to chat to the cute boy/girl two rows forward at break, or who Manchester Utd would draw in the next round of the Cup.

Another reason that you must have notes is that no single textbook will completely cover your syllabus in the way your tutors require it to be covered. This is particularly so in the area of the so-called 'core' subjects, such as Equity, Land and Contract. Many of the recommended texts, for example Chitty on Contracts, are in truth practitioner's texts. Ever in touch with my readers, I hear 'What is a practitioner's text?' I realise that I will have to explain further for you less-than-committed scholars.

A practitioner's text is for people like us, but not until we are in the big bad world do we need to use one. You may now scoff, in your youthful ignorance, and cry that you will *never* use one. But, sadly, you will. In fact, in time, you will actually become quite a hard worker as you realise that your cellar can only be stocked by, and your mortgage can only be paid by, the acquisition of oodles and oodles of loot.

Unless you're lucky enough to make it in the movies (unlikely), happen to be so devastatingly good-looking that people pay thousands to photograph you (even more unlikely), or indeed to be so intelligent that the governments of the world use you as a special adviser (one of my part-time jobs), the only way to get the aforesaid oodles is to work very very hard indeed.

You will then wake up one day and realise that (a) you're 50 years old, (b) you haven't had a laugh in years and are now incredibly dull, and (c) you're about to have a heart attack. But enough of this moralising, and back to practitioner's texts and the avoidance thereof. Doubtless, Cyril and Shirley will have used at least one or more practitioner's texts and will be conversant with both the number of the edition and where it is kept in the library.

The trouble with these books is:

a) they are usually very heavy;

b) they come in more than one part, and if you need Volume 2 you can bet your boots that only Volume 1 is on the shelves; and

c) you have to be extremely clever to use them, as the index is almost indecipherable.

But despair not, help is at hand. I can lead you through this maze. First, you must decide what your aims are, because this will affect the style and content of the notes that you are about to create.

AIMS

I know that this seems to be tempting fate somewhat, but you must decide exactly what you want to achieve in these forthcoming exams. Do I have a choice? I hear you cry. Unless I have very much underestimated the ideal purchaser of this book, then you do have a choice, and a very wide one at that. You have to decide how well, or badly, you want to do. Here are some examples.

(1) The bare pass

Now this has several advantages. There can be no disappointment that you 'only got a 2.2'. If you *do* 'only get a 2.2' then I, along with all your tutors, will be amazed. The bare pass does have a certain amount of panache and style attached to it. After all, you will get the letters after your name (if it is finals' year) and be allowed to stay on at college (if it is another intermediary year). A word of caution here – in some venerable universities, a bare pass means either that you cannot get honours or that you need permission to stay at the university. If this is the case, and as a devotee of my creed I expect you to find out all these details in advance, then you *must* go one higher than a bare pass.

Major words of warning: *never* get involved in one of those 'justify your continued residence here in eight words' meetings in front of four worthy old souls with 3.5 Nobel Prizes between them. They rarely admire the Corinthian spirit, and spent their twenties staring into culture jars, poring over old Greek books, liberating Europe and defeating Hitler. I know, I know – you didn't realise that the Greeks wrote books. (This early devotion to duty on the part of the old souls did pay dividends of a sort. They probably had that first Nobel Prize at the same age you are now.)

So, the bare pass. A little raffish, yet rather cool in a way. Aim for, and get, one of these and you will be thought of as very left-bank. Not by me, though. I shall think you a lazy ... well, just very lazy.

(2)   The bottom-drawer Second

This is not particularly harder to get than a bare pass. In truth, some of those hardy souls attempting to impress their slightly bovine friends with a bare pass often misjudge it and accidentally get a bottom-drawer Second. This can be quite a mishap, and has been known to so effectively demolish an individual's left-bank pretensions that one man, whom I shall call Charlie, in order to restore his credibility, left college at once to live on the aforesaid bank and paint. (Sadly Charlie showed himself to be a true Charlie completely ignorant of down-at-heel style, and set up as a decorator in Battersea. *Left*-bank, Charlie, not *South*-bank.)

The bottom-drawer Second has major disadvantages, however. For one thing, most of the students who achieve these dazzling intellectual heights are those excellent friends of ours, Cyril and Shirley. I pity them, really I do. They try hard, I suppose, but as they said at the dog-track when Gay Muchacho romped home last again, 'You can't put in what God's left out. That's the last time I put ten bob on him each way.' There is therefore nothing worse than getting a bare pass, except aiming for one and getting a bottom-drawer Second. But, if you want to have the chance to be thought a dullard in later life, and perhaps be asked to join the Rotary Club, then aim away .

(3) The polished Second

This is the equivalent of going in to bat at number seven, and dealing with a fresh fast-bowler with style and flourish, before being out for a respectable 42, having saved the follow-on. It means coping with ease, and appearing in the List of Merit in such a position that only those with Firsts do better. In some universities that split their Seconds, this is a good 2.1. (That means that 'Just scraped a 2.1 by the skin of my teeth and which charity should I make the cheque out to, Dean?' types of 2.1 do not count.) It takes ease and charm, and is a very good one to aim for. The only drawback is that if you try and fail, guess what you end up with? Yup, a bottom-drawer. Calamity.

(4) A First

This is the batting equivalent as above, only making 152 not-out in two hours and winning the Test match and hence the Series. Rather obviously, it is extremely difficult, and I do not think more than one or two of you reading this will be capable of it. Some quite bright people will have been trying from last October and will now be fine-tuning their challenge whilst you haven't even started yours yet. However, it can be done and at least if you try and fail there is a good chance that you will end up with a polished Second, and that's not too bad.

Each of the above gets progressively more difficult, and the increase is rather more exponential than arithmetical. A careful and considered choice is needed, because if you choose (4) and then bottle out, you will have only some of the notes you need for a crack at a First, when you should have *all* the (much less impressive) notes for one of the lesser aims. Still, flexibility is the spice of life, as a contortionist I once knew well told me.

I will proceed on the basis that you have chosen either (3) or (4) above. The differences for those interested in (1) and (2) (shame on you) will be pointed out as and when necessary.

Draw up a list of the topics that we discussed in Chapter 2. There should be about ten in all, per paper. You will need to compile notes for each of these topics – a daunting task, but it must be done sooner rather than later. The golden rule is 'garbage in = garbage out', so, unless these notes are full and complete, what chance have your exam answers got? Take a pride in being thorough – you can always choose to omit sub-headings later in the programme.

Use loose-leaf A4 file paper and keep to the same brand. Be generous with your paper. Only write on one side of each sheet. Leave plenty of gaps, which you can supplement later on as you get more and more to grips with this fascinating subject. Keep your notes *tidily* in *separate* A4 files. This is because not only do you not want to look like Cyril and Shirley, but also, from a purely practical point of view, if you leave your file on the bus and it has all your notes in you are in a heck of a worse state than if it only had one-fifth of your notes in there.

Be uniform in your approach to headings, numbering etc. Use new paragraphs as often as you can – it makes the notes more readable later.

Also, and this is purely personal opinion, only use *one* colour ink. There are few sights quite as amusing as watching a Cyril with his five different colours of highlighter, going through photocopies of notes (or cases) until the entire page is a mass of yellow, pink and green. Why do these people do this? What do they think they are achieving? Is it easier to remember a sentence if you splodge through it with a fluorescent pen just after you've read it? They even do it to their own notes!

Apart from anything else, you certainly are a Cyril if you think you are going to be able to use your highlighter supply to good effect in the exam. The most that you can do is to underline case names and statutes in the same colour that you are writing with. It is therefore logical that these are the only artistic embellishments that you should allow yourself.

I suggest black ink, as it looks more impressive against white paper than blue. If you feel like using green or lavender, then change to computer studies at once.

First impressions are tremendously important, as you know. You want to write as well as you can, within the constraints of speed. I therefore *never* used a biro for an exam, as the finished product looks too grotty, with smudges and blotches. I happened to use a fountain pen, but there are very good rolling-ball pens and fibre-tips too. Use whatever makes your writing look best.

Because it is very important to keep absolutely comfortable in every respect in the exam itself, I strongly urge you to write all your notes using the same pen as you will use in the exam. Obviously the smart amongst you will realise that this will not be possible should you be using a non-refillable disposable pen, unless you take notes of a brevity hitherto unsuspected even by those aiming only for a bare pass. Therefore use the same *type* of rolling-ball, that's all, the same *type*.

The next important detail is question-spotting, and the merits thereof. This will be dealt with more fully in the chapter on how to do exam questions. However, all I can say at this stage is do *not* miss out topics at this stage, particularly those end-of-subject topics that no-one takes very seriously because they are covered last, or everyone is revising by the time they come around in lectures. (Not that you would know or care when they are dealt with in lectures, because you never go, do you?)

This is therefore what you need to do, from first principles as it were, to compile yourself a set of notes from scratch. At some time during the academic year, the lecturers and/or the tutors in the subject will have handed out sheets of paper. These were probably handed out at a time when you were thinking of other things, and so you will either have thrown it away or it is in one of your drawers covered in stains because you used it as a coaster for a few weeks.

These sheets of paper are very similar to the lists of cases that are referred to in the next chapter. They contain much useful information, such as chapter numbers in the best textbooks and articles. (More about articles later on.) Unless the lecturers or tutors are impossibly eccentric (always a possibility in Obscure Languages Très Difficiles but less likely in Law) there will be a sheet like this for each subject heading (or tutorial topic). Your task is to acquire a full set of these sheets. Something of a challenge? You bet it is. Because these sheets, that once were so easy to pick up (why, you could have taken a dozen had you been at the lecture) are now very rare indeed.

First port of call is to ask the nerd (there will be a nerd in every faculty or college group of lawyers). You guessed it, the nerd is often called Cyril or Shirley. Hopefully, partly because you are a nice person but also because you are smart and you recognised long ago that the nerd may be of use to you, you will at least be on 'Hello' terms with the nerd. In the early heady days, when people actually spoke to others they didn't know (for a day or two before they got into cliques) you may even have invited the nerd to join you for coffee.

'Cyril, a few of us are going for a cup-au-froth at that new café, The Luscious Trendy. Want to come?'

'I can't. Have you forgotten that there is that supplemental lecture we're allowed to attend on "Legal Ethics in the European Context following 1992"?'

And so on. But you have stayed friendly. Excellent. Ask to look at his notes – he will have these sheets and you can photocopy them. (Whoever invented the photocopier deserves a medal as far as I'm concerned.) If you have not stayed friendly, get friendly. Then borrow and photocopy them.

But the nerd may not have the sheets left, or he may pretend he does not have them because he doesn't want to let *you* have them. Nerds can be like that, a little possessive. I have never worked out why that is. Maybe they resent the fun the rest of us have. Perhaps the little chap has seen through your hollow sham. Well, if he has, you should be ashamed of yourself. Perfect your technique and ask another nerd, you fool. Those sheets are valuable, and you need them. Beg if you have to. Offer a cash payment.

If you are unable to get any, swallow your pride and go and see the lecturer or tutor who handed them out in the first place. I don't care what story you tell him or her. You can confess all (that you are testing the Ten Week Crash Course so you have not done any work yet this year, although you would have loved to) or come up with another transparent little stratagem. I don't care, just *get those sheets*. (Be prepared for sarcastic comments from the academics. Water off a duck's back, mate, water off a duck's back.)

Now you have the sheets in your little paws. Big sigh of relief all round. Using the recommended textbooks and articles, go through and write out all your own notes. This is a major task, and one which will take you a very long time. You must do your very best not to let the whole process take longer than two to three weeks. I know that this will be something of a strain. I know that you will get very unhappy with the drudgery and slowness of the whole thing. However, you really do have only yourself to blame because you have taken it easy for such a long time.

A further difference arises at this point. Those of you aiming (if that is the right word) for a bare pass need only very basic notes, whereas those going for a First will require something very different.

To achieve a First, you must not only be able to deal with the basic foundations of the area of law in the question, you must also be completely able to discuss and refer to much wider areas of the subject, together with policy and other difficult areas. Your notes must, therefore, be very complete. Areas that you miss out when compiling your notes will almost certainly be lost to you for the duration of the ten-week course, and hence you will not be able to refer to those areas or include them in your answers. Thus the task of note creation is so much harder for you if you are trying to do really well in the exams.

The Bare Pass brigade, on the other hand, do not need such Rolls Royce notes. You will only have to satisfy the examiner that you know which exam you are in, to be halfway to a Bare Pass. However, do not take that as carte blanche to come up with an appallingly scrappy set of notes. You must not miss out any areas at all; rather you are entitled just to cover each area in a little less detail, that's all.

These notes, once they are finished, are to be the main source of your knowledge, and so do not be slipshod about them. Make the effort to use the correct textbook, and look up the articles to which you are referred on the sheets. Not all the articles will be of any use – some of them may be on areas too specialised or obscure to fit into your scheme of things – but at least one or two will be of real value. Look at the details of the author, who may be a member of the faculty. If so, and it is a recent article on change in the law, then there is obviously a fighting chance that the topic may come up in the exam. In such circumstances, it is obviously worth your while to learn both the article and the topic to utilise in your own answer. (Word of warning: never *reproduce* the article, or large portions of it, in the exam. You will get little or no credit for it. This is dealt with more fully in the chapter on exam questions.)

Also, although you may borrow the sheets handed out by lecturers and tutors for photocopying, *never ever* photocopy someone else's notes. This is not only dreadfully lazy, but you also miss out on all the background knowledge that you acquire without realising it whilst compiling your own notes. Someone else's notes will not be any use to you anyway, so save your energy. You are going to have to do at least *some* work to get the qualification. Besides, the photocopying charges are enormous, and you cannot pay with a credit card.

Further, there are two different types of notes. These are lecture notes, and notes you make yourself from textbooks, articles, etc (I will call these 'textbook notes'). Now it is possible that, if you are lucky enough to be reading this book at the beginning of the academic year, that you actually have a choice regarding which type of notes you are going to use. More likely, it is already too late for you to start catching up on all the lectures that you have missed (basically a whole year's worth of lectures) so you have no real choice at all.

If you have no choice, despair not. In my opinion, it is a rare lecturer indeed who can provide you with notes on everything you need. Some lecturers actually encourage you to spend the time reading the textbooks because the only people who will receive any benefit from their lectures are those who know what is going on in the subject already. One lecture I went to on Roman Law was held by a lecturer so famously clever it was said that, when an undergraduate himself, he wrote his entire Roman Law exam in Latin. His Roman Law lectures were somewhat difficult to comprehend unless one was an equally impressive scholar. (You are, of course, correct – I had no problem at all following them.) His first lecture did not mention the Romans, or their system of law, at all. Instead, we listened for an hour whilst he lectured on interesting developments in the European Community. Some poor fools thought they were in the wrong lecture, and left. This was great sport for those of us who either understood what was going on, or knew so little about Roman Law that we didn't realise we were not being lectured about it at all.

But back to the point. This lecturer described himself as 'the icing on the cake, the polish on the apple'. (Some fools wrote all this in their notes – shows how selective most people are about what they write in their notes.) Most punters were better off reading the textbooks than listening to him, and he knew it. Most of you *will* be better off using the textbooks, so why bother going to lectures at all? There is little point in duplication, such a waste of your time.

If you want a First, on the other hand, you should of course go to lectures. This is because you will be listening to the people who, apart from having shown themselves to be frightfully clever, are being paid to teach you. If you are aiming for a First then their efforts may not be so wasted as they are on the vast majority of punk rockers. Also, these are the people who will be *marking* your scripts. Listening to them will give you a very good insight into how they are thinking, what developments are important and what you should be paying attention to.

The identity of the lecturer is important, too. You may be lucky enough to have, in your Faculty and ready to lead you through the maze, the well known academic Professor Bloggs. His special field, the co-relationship of the Roman principle of slavery and the Sale of Goods Act of 1979, will probably come up in the exam if he is giving five lectures on it. In any case, if he is that well known, you will always be able to impress interviewers when you finally get around to actually hunting for a job, by calling the Professor by his Christian name and describing what he wore in lectures. So, for that reason alone, it is worth going to at least one lecture.

But if you are not going to use your time in lectures usefully (ie you are going to stare into space for an hour or two and think about generally philosophical things like breakfast) stop fooling yourself and go instead to the library to put in some proper work or to The Luscious Trendy for breakfast and a cup-au-froth.

If you *are* going to go to lectures, then be selective about what you write down. This is for two reasons. Firstly, the human voice can speak much quicker than most human hands can write. You do not want your hand to drop off. (I have heard of someone to whom this happened, though the story may be purely apocryphal.) Secondly, there are those who would write down the entire bus timetable if the lecturer read it out. They write down 'Good morning' when the lecturer says 'Good morning'. They are fools, and imagine the amount of rubbish they have to wade through come revision time. Besides, their names are Cyril and Shirley and you don't want to end up like them, now, do you?

4

CASES AND STATUTES

CASE-LAW

Law students are by no means unique. You will all, I hope, know colleagues and fellow travellers who spend their time studying (or not studying) subjects as wide-ranging as English Literature (identifiable by the black berets some of them sport), Obscure Languages Très Difficiles (not quite as difficile for some as for others) and Medicine. [Medics (particularly the males) are, as you all know, extremely uncouth and rough so avoid them.] In a way, all students and most subjects are very similar, and revising for one is similar to revising for another.

However, there is one fundamental difference when it comes to the study of the law. Law is essentially a system for everyday use – this is difficult to appreciate when you are reading about Semi-Secret Trusts and whether the testator could validly leave the family silver to his pack of foxhounds – and, as such, the area that you are studying at any one time will have cropped up at some time earlier. That knotty question will have been discussed before, even if it was only obiter dicta in *Jarndyce* v *Jarndyce*.

Walk into any law library anywhere in the world, and that aspect of the subject that has terrified so many in the past (and will continue to do so) will be staring down at you from the shelves: The Law Reports, containing that wondrous aspect of judicial analysis and judgment, the case-law. (Statutes are dealt with at the end of this chapter.)

There will be new books and old books, some well-thumbed volumes and others covered in dust, but they will each contain a great deal of very useful stuff, and that is the stuff of success. By the end of this chapter, this will be at your fingertips, another weapon in your fight for exam superiority.

You will learn more golden rules in this chapter, but the first is that you must *not* allow case-law to frighten you. I have met people who were put off studying law whilst still at school because they were told how difficult it was to learn 'all those cases'. This really is dreadful. (What? Learning all the cases or being put off law altogether?) Learning cases is no harder than learning any other long, dreadfully turgid, quite confusing, ill-planned – but I forget myself, I am here to fill you with confidence and daring. Learning cases is quite straightforward and should not daunt even the faintest heart.

Before you learn the cases, however, you must understand them. Then you can decide how many and which ones it is worth your precious time to learn in the first place.

I was always amused, as so often when watching the fools at play, to see the Cyrils and Shirleys of the world sitting in the library in those early autumn mornings (I would be on my way to buy croissants at that well know eaterie, the library croissant shop) with the accoutrement they fondly believe is essential to the understanding of case-law, The Card-Index File.

I have no idea why they feel that one of these is necessary. I once watched a Cyril for some time (a long queue for croissants that day) whilst he busied himself with his task for the morning. This appeared to involve looking up a case, and then copying some short part of it onto the card from The Card-Index File, which was sitting next to him.

This task was repeated again and again, and you can imagine my amazement. What was he doing? Why had he bought The Card-Index File in the first place? Where had he found that list of cases, which seemed to go on for ever? And, more importantly, was he in the queue for croissants?

Cyril the young hearty was then to be spied in the revision period with the plethora of cards in his hands as though he were practising for a game of 44-card poker. He then shuffled them again and again, looking down from time to time and then closing his eyes. All the while he had a look of anguish across his ... well, ugly features. And then, come the exam, he was carried sobbing from the room after answering two partial questions on the Highland Clearances. (Yes. He had gone into the History exam by mistake and not realised.)

You will obviously not follow his poor example. The way to demolish a case is to obey the following sequence:

a)   reading;
b)   understanding;
c)   writing
d)   learning;
e)   revising;
f)   using.

We will consider each element in turn in detail.

Reading

The initial step is to decide which case to look up in the first place. Any particular case must have been mentioned somewhere for you to know that it exists at all. It may have been mentioned in lectures (in which case how you got to hear of it remains a mystery) or contained in one of those lists that supervisors and tutors love so much.

These lists, well known to all of us who have battled against the tutor (you know, the sort who believes that hard work starts at the beginning of the autumn term), are usually incredibly long and daunting. The problem is often the tutor himself (or herself) and the fact that the reason that the person is teaching you at all is because he (or she) is An Academic.

An Academic. Think about it for a moment. Love of the subject, be it Equity and Trusts or even (incredibly) those bizarre subjects like Landlord and Tenant or Planning Law, a deep and thorough understanding, coupled with something of an intellect, have marked your tutor out as a true academic guide. And here you are, reading *this*! What a contrast.

The problem for you is that you end up with a list of cases that could be either essential or completely inconsequential, and you will not know which until you look them up (and you have not enough time to look them all up). Some tutors helpfully put an asterisk or other mark next to the *essential* cases on their lists, and leave the committed to research the rest of them. That sort of tutor is, sadly, rare.

The short cut is relatively straightforward. If the subject that you are studying has a *casebook*, use that for all the cases contained therein. Casebooks contain an admirably cogent analysis of the particular case and will isolate parts of the judgment that you really *ought* to read, for example Lord Atkin's 'neighbour' principle in *Donoghue* v *Stevenson*.

However, if no up-to-date casebook exists (or you do not have access to one) then look through the case-index of the most recent edition of the recommended textbook in that subject. (Word of warning: *never use an out-of-date textbook*. It is a ridiculous risk and will show you up in an appalling light should that area of law deployed by you in the exam have changed. And if you refer to any particular case, you can bet your bottom dollar that it *will* have been over-ruled.)

Go through the index and tick off on your list any case that is dealt with in the textbook. You will then, whilst using the textbook to create your notes, deal with those cases mentioned in it and can look them up further should you want to. You also ensure that you do not miss out on any important cases that, for whatever reason, are *not* mentioned in the textbook. Sounds simple? Well, better get started, hadn't you?

You now know what cases you are going to have to look up. As you know, the Law Reports come in different types – the All England Reports, the Weekly Law Reports, the Times Law Reports and the Lloyd's Law Reports, to name but a few. I advise you to try to keep to one type when there is a choice – you will grow used to the reporter's style – but they are uniformly excellent. Do not make the mistake of thinking that because a case is reported in the Times or Independent Law Reports, it is not in the 'proper' law reports and you can therefore miss it out.

These newspaper reports, as well as being very good (the Independent in particular has *excellent* reports – can I have a free subscription?), have the added advantage that they are most recent, usually being reported within a few days of the actual judgment being given. Even the best loose-leaf reports are, inevitably, somewhat out-of-date by comparison because the report only comes out every month (or whatever the particular interval is).

For example, the recent House of Lords judgment in *Murphy* v *Brentwood District Council* that over-ruled *Anns* v *London Borough of Merton* appeared in the daily papers on 23 July 1990, much sooner than in the Law Reports themselves. (If you didn't know that *Anns* v *London Borough of Merton* was no longer good law, go to the bottom of the class forthwith or, preferably, change to computer studies.)

Similarly, do not avoid looking up cases that happen to appear in the more unusual reports like the Lloyd's Law Reports. These are usually cases reported from either the Commercial or Admiralty Court, or from the Court of Appeal on appeal from those Courts, and are very useful in the field of contract, insurance and suchlike.

Should you be studying International Trade or something like that then you will find these reports essential. They have the added advantage of being, for the most part, substantially shorter than the more widespread reports. To someone like you, this means that there is the chance of reaping a dividend out of proportion to the degree of extra effort required.

When you read a case, read the headnote first very carefully so that you can discern exactly what the case is about. There is little point reading a case that you think is about easements, which takes you eight pages to realise that the judge is in fact talking about mortgages. However, do not fool yourself that you can read only the headnote, copying that out and resting content that you have read the case. You will not have done, and you must not rely on the headnote in that manner.

(Do not bother yourself with reading the arguments of Counsel in those reports that reproduce such details. Although these are very interesting, their purpose is not to distract undergraduates for 30 minutes, most of whom will not have a clue what the co-relation between waiver and estoppel is, and the exam will not require such knowledge.)

Go on and read the leading judgment once, without taking notes. If there is more than one judgment, which means the case will be an appellate decision, then the others will often be quite short. Some will simply say 'I agree' in more or less those terms. If there are *dissenting* judgments, then I recommend that you read them because it is all useful grist to the mill to show off your knowledge later.

Think to yourself: what is this about? Could you confidently and clearly explain the case to someone else? If not, then read it again. Once you understand it, write out on a piece of A4 the full heading and reference, a brief summary of the facts and the gist of the judgment. I always found it useful to set the points of the judgment out in numbered fashion; that helped me to realise if I had missed something out when it came to the exam.

Points to note: If you have not studied much law before, you will be amazed when you read your first case. It will be confusing and difficult. Cases do not resemble textbook style at all. This is because a case is a real dispute about real problems, and these are rarely nicely packaged into discrete areas of the law. You may well have to wade though a great quantity of what seems, to you, to be irrelevant detail. Do not be put off, however. Eventually you will get the knack of it, except perhaps in the field of Equity. Does anyone understand Equity?

Understanding

You should have accomplished at least some of this by following the section on Reading. Read through the case as many times as you need to understand it – use the test of explaining it to someone, even yourself, out loud. You must now place that piece of knowledge, as well as that piece of paper with the details written on, in your notes. This is one of the reasons that I told you earlier in the book to use loose-leaf paper and files. Just slot it in there. Write a reference to it in the text of your notes (remember that you left lots of gaps?) and you can see, I hope, that the whole campaign is beginning to take shape.

If you do *not* understand any case, or a particular aspect of a case, then do not worry. It is nothing to be ashamed of, and do not be reluctant to admit it, unless you are completely bovine. I still do not fully understand *Re Vandervell's Trusts*. The best thing to do if something is unclear is to ask one of your friends doing the same subject – the opinion of Matt the Medic may be very interesting but it is not going to help you much.

Anyone who is *unwilling* to help you out, scratch them off the list straight away. Knowledge is not something to be kept from others, and you are not in this in competition with the others in your group or even in the Faculty. This is between three of you – you, the exam, and the examiner. Sadly, Law in particular appears to attract some people with an appalling Paper Chase mentality, and once you realise who they are then avoid them.

If all else fails, go to see your tutor in that subject. Barring the odd sarcastic comment, even the most academic of them all will be more than happy to explain something, and it is best to make sure that you understand as much as you can before the real aggro starts in the exam. There will be enough going on without your having an 'Oh no, I *knew* I should have sorted that out' nightmare in the first question.

Writing

In the exams, and in fact in the law in general, cases are important because you use them as an authority for a principle or proposition. Time is tight in most exams – you usually have to do four or five questions in three hours. That does not give you much time to recite the facts in *Bloggs* v *Bloggs* at great length, together with your views on the learned Judge's deep understanding about maintenance payments. This will be dealt with in much greater depth in the chapter on how to answer exam questions, but you must distill from the case a single, or perhaps two, principles that will succinctly fit into place if the situation merits it. Here is an example.

> In law, a man owes his neighbour a duty of care such that he must not, by doing an act or omitting to do an act, thereby cause his neighbour harm; *Donoghue* v *Stevenson*.

Now this is, of course, an extremely easy and, in a way, unfair example because it is so well known. But note the form. This principle and case name, taken from your notes, can be adapted to fit almost any negligence problem or essay question in the Law of Tort exam.

It comprises the principle, that of tortious recovery, with the authority, the case name. Now of course not all the cases that you studiously prepare and include in your notes will be as useful as the one above, and many may not come up at all. Some will be authority for particular sets of circumstances that do not come into the problem questions at all.

Write each of these distilled principles at the foot of the text written about the case on that sheet of A4 you inserted in your notes.

But you should not look on what is *not* used as wasted work, not by any means. For one thing, any cases that you do retain (we shall discuss later memory and percentage of retention) can be used to illustrate points in any essay questions that you attempt. Such questions, although they have their disadvantages, do offer you a little more scope to get some return on all that information locked away in your head.

Secondly, and this is going to win me the Cyril award for stating the obvious, you do not know what is going to appear in the exam until you have sat down and read the paper on the dreadful day itself. So in the best traditions of the Boy Scout movement ('Be Prepared'), distill from each case on the list (and therefore now in your notes) one or two principles and save them for later.

Learning and revising

You must be able to rely on, and that means quote, the cases' names, as well as the principles distilled from them, in the exam. This means that you will have to be carrying an enormous amount of data in your head when you sit in front of the exam paper, so you can retrieve and use it at will.

The process of actually learning such a large volume of raw facts comes more easily to some than to others, but if you are one of those people who find it difficult, do not be downhearted. You can be helped with this, as you can be helped with all your other academic difficulties (!). (Illiteracy, however, I cannot help you with.)

The first thing to do is to ensure that you only bother learning what is worthwhile. This is one of the reasons behind my earlier instruction to distill the relevant principles from those cases that you have studied. These principles should not be too verbose, and since the formulation of them is a task that you will accomplish on your own, the wording and style of them will be familiar.

As the exam approaches, go through all your notes on a particular subject and write, all on one sheet of paper (or two or three, depending on how many cases there were for that subject) the case names and the principles, in column form. This shortened case list will then form part of your revision notes for that subject.

There is no need to use the whole case citation in the exam in the same way that you would use for an essay. This therefore means that you do not need to learn those details. The year in which the case was reported, and the report reference itself, are irrelevant for exam purposes. I am not sure that an exam marking system exists for rewarding the stupidity of a candidate who goes to the bother of learning all that extra detail.

Also, it is acceptable to make some sensible abbreviations of the names of the parties themselves. This means that you can shorten long names of companies. You are not being given extra marks for the accuracy of knowing that *Westerbury Property* v *Carpenter* is in reality called *Westerbury Property and Investment Company Ltd* v *Carpenter*.

Additions to the name such as 'Limited' and its German equivalent, 'Gmbh', can be ignored. Cases involving ships, usually to be found in the Lloyds' Law Reports, will often also be given the name of the ship itself, and this appears after the names of the parties. This appears in the Reports themselves, so it is obviously an approved practice. These cases are referred to in this way in Court, as well.

Be sensible. As long as the examiner can tell that you know which case you are talking about, and you have identified the name correctly, then you will receive credit for it. Thus the task of learning the turgid lists of cases becomes slightly less daunting when you see what proportion of the detail has to be retained, and what proportion can be ignored.

So: *Services Europe Atlantique Sud SEAS* v *Stockholms Rederiaktiebolag SVEA, The Folias* [1979] AC 685 becomes, simply, *The Folias*; *National Westminster Bank plc* v *Arthur Young McClelland Moores and Company* [1985] 1 WLR 1123 becomes *NatWest Bank* v *Arthur Young*; and so on.

You can see that, in this way, the amount that you have to actually take on board is reduced before you even start.

Please do not labour under that sad misapprehension that you *should* learn all these details because, 'if I start cutting corners now, I will be putting my entire future at risk' and, indeed, will spend eternity stoking the central heating system in Beelzebub's utility room. I knew one person who, as a concession, only learnt the *year* in which the case was reported instead of the entire citation. He succeeded in doing so. But just consider the wasted effort, and wasted time, that he could have used to do something else instead. All that brain power down the tubes.

There is a lot more to the law than learning cases, and I doubt if any of the examiners will even notice that you have recited the entire title, the names of the Counsel who appeared and the birthday of the Judge.

On the contrary, and this applies particularly to cases in the House of Lords and the Court of Appeal, if you are aiming for a First and if you *can* remember the name of one or two of the judges who sat in the case, and the gist of one or two of their sentences, then this does generate credit and should be considered. Any of you aiming for a First should *certainly* do this, because it is not possible to do really well in an essay question unless you have this depth of knowlege. The degree of return you will get will be out of proportion to the effort that you will expend, and so it is of course worth doing.

After the task of writing out all the *essential* details is done, then you will have a ready-made aide memoire for the very dull task of hammering it home. There are no short cuts to this; it is a question of reading through it time and again, with periodic testing sessions of one sort or another to see how much you have retained. Without question, you will remember the cases better should you actually understand the case, so be certain not to embark on the learning process until you have mastered the rudiments of the cases themselves.

As far as the self-testing process is concerned, some people find that they retain detail better if they write it out again and again. I do not think it better to use one system over another – it is really a matter of personal choice; however you should have a variety of different testing systems. This will help to prevent terminal boredom setting in, and ensure that you do not only use one system because that is the one that you are best at.

Provided you are adhering to the timetable and assuming that you have not taken too long to actually compile your notes, you should not be ready to use your shortened case list much before the time when there is three weeks or less to go to the first exam. Essentially all your list is, is a more useful version of the one that all the lecturers handed out in the first week of term, with your distilled principles replacing the citation details that I have told you it is not worth learning.

Further, you will have the added advantage of actually knowing which cases are the *really* useful ones, and you will also have a background of knowledge from having read the cases through and made notes.

You would be surprised how much knowledge can end up locked in your head without your really trying to put it there. With a little bit of luck, you will find that, once you are sitting in the exam and writing out the appropriate principle and case, a little piece of information may pop into your mind, having been placed there through a thorough understanding of the case.

It may be a sentence from the judgment, it may even be a decision of the American or Commonwealth Courts to which the judge refers, but you will be pleasantly surprised if it does happen and it will do you no harm. Particularly regarding decisions from overseas, you will (rightly) be given enormous credit for this impressive piece of scholarship.

Using

The way in which you put your accumulated case-law depends very much upon what subject you are studying, and the type of question you are attempting, whether essay-type or problem-type. For example, in Jurisprudence or Legal History the need to have such a formidable array of principles/case names is likely to be far less important than in a subject such as Land Law, which is practically all case-law and statutes.

(For Equity, you will need to write down all that you know about the subject, and that will take you approximately 25 minutes. After that, you will have to amuse yourself for two and a half hours, so ask if you can take in a novel to read after all the screamers have left the room and hence ceased to entertain you.)

The differences in approach are covered more completely in the chapter dealing with those two different types of question, but it is broadly correct that essay questions will require a greater knowledge of the decision than that contained in your shortened case list. So, if a question is all about one particular case and all you know about it is that it is recent and you *meant* to read it, honestly you did, then move on to the next question.

STATUTES

These are more difficult, and your approach will depend on the particular rules at your seat of learning. Some Faculties permit unmarked copies of the relevant statutes to be taken into the examination room. Worthy individuals will then walk around the room during the exam (undoubtedly wearing new shoes that creak and make other bizarre noises) and, sporadically, swoop on the statute book of an unsuspecting examinee and check that it has not been marked with helpful hints. (This can cause a degree of shock to the unsuspecting examinee. An involuntary cry or seizure of some sort due to the sudden drop in blood pressure can provide you with untold entertainment.) There are several points to note here.

a) Usually only certain editions of the relevant statutes are permitted, and you must ensure that you buy one of the approved versions. Check with your tutor or in the exam regulations (these are, as you can imagine, a really riveting read), and don't be a dummy and get the wrong sort. In some faculties, not even the HMSO versions are approved; you have to have the relevant book published by certain publishers. I have never been able to ascertain why this is, but logic plays little part in exams.

b) If you *are* allowed to take in statutes, then make sure that you do actually take some in. It is an absolute waste and appallingly lazy not to bother at all because you didn't buy any or cannot be bothered to borrow some. And if you are of the opinion that you cannot afford them, then spend a little less of your grant or allowance on beer and a little more on books. It will be money well spent, I promise you.

If you are not allowed to use statutes in any particular subject, then this may be because statutes are not relevant, or it may be because the faculty want to ensure that your time is really wasted and you will have to learn all the relevant section numbers. It depends on the subject in question.

Some subjects, like Land Law, are practically all statute-based. There is a statute in Land Law known as the Law of Property Act 1925. For some reason, in 1925 the legislators in their wisdom passed lots of statutes about Land Law, but the Law of Property Act 1925 is the biggest and best. (If you have been studying Land Law all year and have not heard of the Law of Property Act of 1925, I suggest you change to computer studies as soon as possible. They may not have you, though, which shows just how dreadful you must be.)

This statute is essential to the Land Law exam, and all the section numbers of the most exciting and innovative provisions will need to appear in your exam answers. If they do not appear, then a Bare Pass for you (at best!). So that means, if you are not permitted statutes, you must learn all the section numbers. And do not be impressed by colleagues of yours who say that it is unnecessary to learn the precise number of the section etc. You can bet your bottom dollar that *they* will be secretly learning all that detail late at night in order to gain an unfair advantage over you. So, if this happens to you, smile and agree with them and stick to the plan.

NB The reason that some people are able to try to pull this trick is because they were at the lecture when the Deputy Sub-Head of the Faculty Examination and Senate Regulatory Sub-Committee put in an appearance to tell all the happy little punters what the rules were regarding statutes. Of course, *you* were not at that lecture because you were at the bakery/coffee shop trying a particularly delicious Danish pastry with your cappuccino.

But back to the statutes. The way to learn the section numbers (if you have to do so) is to adapt the case learning system slightly. Write down all the numbers on one side of a piece of A4 and précis the section on the other side (ensuring of course that the précis is opposite the correct section number or you'll learn all the *wrong* numbers). I apologise for having to provide such basic details, which I know must frustrate all you Nobel Prize winners, but I have to cater for all sorts, even undergraduates from Oxford.

If you are lucky enough not to need to learn the numbers, and you are organised enough to purchase the correct edition of the statutes from the approved publisher, then you have to decide how much time you are likely to have on your hands during the exam itself.

It may be that you will be so hard-pressed for anything helpful or sensible to say that you will not mind having a minute or two off to leaf through your statute book in a leisurely fashion, trying to find section 143(8)(viii). However, should that be an unlikely scenario (and not so unlikely as you may think), then you can save yourself a little bit of time in advance. You need a quantity of those little yellow flags that have adhesive (sticky stuff to those at Oxford) on one half so you can flag pages easily and write the section number so that it is clearly visible. Spend an afternoon going through the statute book in this way and Hey Presto! Valuable minutes saved in the exam itself.

But beware not to write anything else on the little flag, not even 'Spurs for the Cup', because (a) Spurs are probably not going to win the Cup again this century, and (b) the worthy individual swooping down in the exam will notice, grab your script from before you, and scream 'You low-down no-good cheating scum-bag!' before tearing it into a thousand pieces. Not very cool at all, for either of you, but remember he has checked thousands of statute books and never found anything written there that shouldn't have been, so don't be too harsh. He has been planning that reaction for some years.

And, of course, the best uses for statute books include something to read when you have run out of things to write down in the exam, and providing handy sheets of paper to tear out and put under the desk leg, to stop the desk rolling like a North Sea trawler every time you write a word.

5
THE EXAMS THEMSELVES

So now we come onto the actual exams themselves. The dreadful days, some of you may think. This is, of course, completely the wrong approach, and you *must* get your mental approach right if you are to do yourself justice.

The whole aim of the plan so far has been to prepare you for the coming onslaught. Knowledge and preparedness is power, and this is why, if you are reading this chapter without having correctly followed all the steps to date, then you are selling yourself short. What is the point of spending time in higher education, if you are not even going to make an effort to pass the exams? Get your act together pronto.

However, most of you will, I hope, be reading this *after* having got your notes in order, preparing your case lists and generally gearing up for a fair attempt at these minor little tests.

In most examination systems, your performance on the day is the one that will make or break you. As you all know, very few universities and polytechnics have the sort of system that requires you to work throughout the year, continually assessing your progress. Indeed, it is because of this that my system can work at all. There is little point in planning a ten-week blitz of a campaign, when by Easter you have lost 75 per cent of the available marks because you took three months off to study wildlife in Guadaloupe.

The converse of this is that you will get little reward in the long run if you enter the exam hall knowing the subject backwards, but have such a nightmare three hours that all your expertise is wasted and not transferred to your script.

Now there are numerous philosophical points of view regarding which system is fairer, or more appropriate, to find out how dashed clever you really are. I will not enter into such arguments here; suffice it to say that you are stuck with the old 'performance on the day' routine and hence that is the one that you must ensure you succeed at.

It will be no comfort to you when you cannot find a job to say 'Well, if it had only been continual assessment I would have done much better, ie I'd have actually passed my exams.' There would not *be* exams if there was continual assessment – you are just showing up your ignorance.

Thus your entire three hours for that paper must be spent demonstrating (a) how well you have understood the question and what superb analytical skills you have, and (b) how firm your grasp of the subject is. You must at all times remember that, no matter how much you know, how many cases etc you fully understand, you have to let the examiner in on the secret or he/she is going to think you are a biff. Let me explain the ground rules to do with technique itself, which should be obvious to you anyway.

FULLY READ, AND COMPLY WITH, ALL THE INSTRUCTIONS

This is the first thing you must do. Particularly in compulsory and core subjects in law exams, the paper will be split into sections. For those of you who think this is so simple that I am re-inventing the wheel, consider this. These instructions are by no means always simple. It may be the first exam you have taken at university. You may feel stressed. Your brain may feel it is about to burst, it has so much information in it. (Unlikely, but there's always hope!)

There may be a compulsory essay question. There may be a section made up entirely of essay questions, of which you must answer at least one, but are not permitted to answer more than two. If it is a split paper, for example Sale of Goods and Consumer Credit, there will certainly be provisions regarding the number of questions you must answer for each topic.

You may have to answer each question on a fresh piece of paper. You may have two different answer books, one for each section. You may be required to write only on one side of the paper. Penalties will exist in the marking scheme for non-compliance with, or breaches of, these instructions, particularly the ones regarding how many from each section or compulsory questions. Let me tell you a salutory story.

I know a woman who was very clever and worked very hard. She wanted a First. She had achieved a First in her Part 1 of Tripos, and if she managed a First in the exams in her last year she would have achieved a most impressive goal. She knew everything and was extremely bright. Now, to get a First, you need very good performances in *all* your papers. One booby paper and you're finished. She was taking a paper in Labour Law, and this was split into two sections. This was her last paper, and the others had gone very well. In Labour Law, she answered five good questions, and walking back to College after the exam she was glancing through her exam paper and her world completely fell in. This was not because a workman dropped a brick on her from a ladder. No, it was because she noticed that she had omitted to answer the minimum two questions from section 1. The infuriating thing was, she could have *easily* answered the other one, she knew the topic etc. She blew it. Her mark in that paper was not good enough, and she just missed that First.

In such circumstances, the examiner will only mark you on the four questions that you answered, in accordance with the rules. What else can they do? The rules are there for a reason, and so at least 20 per cent of all the available marks in that paper may be completely unobtainable *if you do not follow the instructions*. You will therefore forgive me if I labour the point. It can happen to anybody – *make sure that it does not happen to you*.

ALWAYS ANSWER THE FULL NUMBER OF QUESTIONS REQUIRED

Again, this must be obvious, but so many candidates blow even this simple little rule and suffer the consequences. 'Oh, I was doing quite well but I just ran out of time.' What an idiot is the person who says such a thing. Everyone knows before they go into the exam hall how long the exam will last. If they don't know before they get in, it appears at the top of every exam paper I have ever seen. Each candidate knows, again almost certainly before they go into the exam hall, how many questions they must answer. So why do so many people get it wrong?

Pure stupidity. This is closely tied in with the law of diminishing returns, discussed below, but no-one is going to give you credit for one absolutely wonderful answer, two partial answers and two missing answers because you 'ran out of time'. A great many candidates, particularly in their first exam, are convinced that they need to produce really excellent answers. Of course, the more excellent the answer then the better the mark is going to be *for that question*. But, if you are required to answer five questions, then you must balance the excellence of your answers with the time allowed.

If you are in a three-hour exam, you have only an average of *thirty-five minutes* per question. Thirty-five minutes is not very long at all. Further, thirty-five minutes per question only give you five minutes in hand overall. So all those people who pile enthusiastically into their first question and spend an hour and a half on it are inevitably ruining their chances, although they think they are really producing a rather special answer.

As you become more experienced, and depending on how cool you are in the heat of the exam, you can of course carry time not used in one answer (perhaps on a topic in which you are less strong) onto another answer. As long as you do not *average* less than thirty-five minutes a question, it does not matter. The best use of exam technique will result in your finishing your last question about two minutes before the invigilator shouts 'Stop writing now, you worthless academic offal' or similar words that adequately reflect his opinion of your pigmy intellect.

The best aid to good time-keeping, in my opinion, is to write the times down as soon as you are allowed to write anything. You will of course have a watch or be able to see a clock. (If due to some mishap you do not have a watch with you, or you cannot see a clock, then at the start ask the examiner or adjudicator for one. You should at the very least be able to see one on the wall.) On a piece of paper, write down the start time and the exact time on from that in 35-minute intervals. The reason for doing this is your mind *should* be fully occupied during the exam thinking about all sorts of legal things. It is only going to distract you if you are constantly doing mental calculations in modulus 35 using the 24-hour clock.

Although I have said that unused time for one question *can* be carried on to another (on a topic where you are stronger or more confident), I do not suggest that you spend less than thirty minutes on any single question. The reason for this is that, although you may think that you are completely finished on that question after twenty minutes, you may think up something else if you give yourself a few extra minutes. Any extra marks on that question will come easier than at the end of another question in which you have already written a great deal (the law of diminishing returns).

DO NOT SPEND VALUABLE MINUTES AT THE START OF THE EXAM DOING MENIAL TASKS

Such tasks of a menial nature include writing your name or number on the top of the paper or on the cover sheet, filling in the details about the title of the paper, etc. You will be permitted to do these things at the very end, after you have been told to stop writing. Why waste time when you could be gaining extra marks? You may spend seven or eight minutes doing such things at the very beginning of the exam. These minutes may be very precious to you at the end of the three hours.

One final point. I do not think that, in law exams, there is much point in allowing yourself 'time for checking' at the end. I know that some people recommend it, but what can you really usefully check? The only thing worth doing at the end is, perhaps, checking the case names or filling in gaps you have left for case names that have slipped out of your mind in the heat of battle. It is not like some exams in other subjects that include calculations in which you may have made a mistake that you will discover on checking. I would use your time more fruitfully in the answering of other questions themselves first time round.

QUESTION SPOTTING – IS IT WORTH DOING?

This now brings me to that esoteric art – attempting to guess or otherwise ascertain what the questions are actually going to be. This is a very controversial technique, yet some people do seem to be able to do it with great success. Is it just luck? Should you have a go?

The first thing to realise is that not only is it very risky but it will not provide you with more than one or two questions at the most. So do not use it as a substitute for actually learning and revising the subject properly.

However, it would be foolish to ignore any clues or hints that are available regarding the areas to be examined on. Each subject is potentially vast, and to concentrate on a narrower field is sensible, if that narrow field is to come up in the exam.

A sensible way to start is to look at your lecture syllabus. This is because there is a very good chance that one of the lecturers will have had a large amount to do with the setting of the paper itself. You could ask your tutor or supervisor who is setting the paper. He or she may tell you; more likely they will not know or will not be allowed to pass on the information. Try not to bribe your tutor too obviously, but do keep your ears open for any hints. Academics are, by definition, very clever and he or she may just drop the odd cryptic comment that, with a bit of thought, will give the game away. It can be a little like talking to a living, speaking crossword puzzle.

If you do find out who is setting the paper, then find out what his or her specialist interests are. Look him or her up in the good law journals to see if he or she has written any articles. If so, read them. If any of them are in the field in which that person is lecturing you, then you do not have to be a Nobel Prize winner to realise that there is a good chance that the subject may come up in the exam. This is particularly so if the article is regarding a recent major change in the law, or happens to coincide with a series of four or five lectures on that topic.

The other rich source of hints is the collection of past exam papers. With any luck the library or faculty will have a set of these, and you will be permitted to photocopy them. If not, then there are publications that include former exam papers together with suggested solutions. If you have one of these publications, then for exam-spotting purposes ignore the suggested solutions for the moment.

Look through these past papers. (This is also a good way of getting the feel of what style the paper is, what sections it is in and what the usual instructions are.)

Make a list of the topics that have come up over the past six or seven years. There may very well be a particularly hoary old chestnut that appears again and again. If a question has come up for the last three or four years, then it may well come up again. (Word of warning, and this is what makes question-spotting so risky. The fact that a question has come up for the past three or four years may very well make it more likely that it *will not* come up this year, because the examiners have got tired of it.)

You will get a taste of the sort of question that is likely. I remember, when studying for my exam in Roman Law, that in the past papers there always seemed to be questions about objects falling from, or being thrown out of, windows onto passers-by. Now and again, the poor passer-by would be a slave. So I looked into this tricky area.

In the exam itself, imagine my desolation and despair (chuckle, chuckle) when I opened the exam paper to find that there was in fact a question all about an Inn-sign falling onto a genial traveller called Marcus. This happened at the same time as a flower pot was thrown from an upper window, sadly hitting not Marcus but his slave.

Oh dear oh dear, I thought. I am just going to have to answer that question.

And the final rule, dealt with more fully under damage limitation:

NEVER PANIC – KEEP YOUR HEAD AT ALL TIMES

... even if all appears to be going dreadfully wrong and, after forty minutes of angst, you are convinced that you can do nothing at all. In fact, you are tempted to run screaming from the exam hall. Do not indulge your sense of the dramatic in such a pathetic way. You will only be providing entertainment for people like me, happily tucking into my second question.

Even if you find that you cannot think of how to begin, and your mind is a complete blank, do not worry. Just start writing; anything really, it doesn't matter. Even a letter to your dear old Gran.

You are not there to produce a beautifully polished essay or problem question that is going to win you prizes from journals, impressed with your style. (Of course, if you can do so then that is a bonus.) No, you are there to turn out good, reasonable answers that will get you credit in the exam. Your first sentence does not have to be of Chekovian profundity.

Another little story. I was in an exam once (Law of Tort, as I remember) and a jolly difficult exam it was too. Of the ten questions that we had to choose from, there were about eight all about the law of negligence. A poor soul near to me sat, despairing, attempting to write his first question. He would stare into space (obviously searching for the inspiration that I have already told you will rarely come) and then write down a sentence. He would then stare into space again, before looking back down at his sentence already written. He would then tear up that piece of paper and repeat the process. He must have written the first sentence at least a dozen times. What a waste of time. During all the time that he was spending trying to construct an excellent opening, the clock was ticking away and his chances of success were fading.

You *must* start writing. You will find that the very act of doing that will unlock a lot of your knowledge, and probably even relax you as well. You can always go back later and change the beginning if you want to. If it is a letter to the Gran, then I suggest you *do* change it.

FOCUS ON YOUR STRONG AREAS AND DEAL WITH YOUR WEAK ONES

It is of course axiomatic that you will, within any one subject, have areas that you are good at, and areas that you are not so good at. If you are unlucky, you may also have areas that you are absolutely dreadful at, but we will try not to dwell on that depressing aspect. You may also be very ugly, but we will try not to dwell on that, either.

It is obvious that you need to iron out the weak areas, so that if you are forced by circumstances to answer questions on the weak areas you do not completely botch it up. The reason that you *are* good at certain subjects is you enjoy those subjects, whether consciously or subconsciously. Because you do enjoy those topics, the temptation is to concentrate on them in your revision. You must revise *all* the topics contained in your revision lists, which as you remember are taken from the lecture and tutorial syllabus notes. So, whether you enjoy the issue of Land Law reform necessary to protect the interest of a non-working spouse in the marital home or not, you have to wade through it none the less. If you don't enjoy it you will probably have to spend *even* more time on it to make sure all the detail is being retained.

However, yet another word of warning. You must strike a balance between concentrating on your weak topics (to get them up to standard) and not neglecting the strong subjects. Just knowing the broad detail of your favourite topic is not enough, you must be able to provide a good answer in the exam. Keep a weather eye on the development of your weak areas, and if the balance shifts because you've spent a week doing all the topics that you hate, redress it with a crash course on all the things you enjoy. (That does *not* mean a crash course on inebriation because you enjoy it.)

THE LAW OF DIMINISHING RETURNS

This is very simple, and concerns the degree of credit that is available for any particular amount of work, in relation to the effort required to gain that extra credit. It is a law very well known to all those whose school reports included the criticism 'Little Jimmy does just enough to get by.'

Translated, this means that little Jimmy knew the law of diminishing returns very well and we can all learn from his expertise. This is not to say that I am encouraging you to do 'just enough to get by'. Far from it. Only those foolhardy souls trying to gauge a Bare Pass will be laying themselves open to the criticism that they are only doing 'just enough to get by'. As I have explained, that is the aim of a Bare Pass in the first place, and we have already gone into all that earlier.

However, there is a distinction between doing just enough to get by, and spending hours on an essay when you have achieved 99 per cent of the marks available in the first three pages.

When you are doing an essay for a tutorial, or to hand in during the year, it is your own time you are wasting and, if you want to spend an extra week doing an essay to perhaps gain one or two extra marks, then that is your affair. I will think you a fool, but it really is a matter for you. It does demonstrate a remarkable lack of judgment, though.

In the exams themselves, though, it is a different matter entirely. All those minutes spent fine-tuning your eight-page answer, so polished it would do credit to an academic journal, are minutes that you should spend gaining other marks on another question.

It is more likely that you will make this mistake if you have been spending your academic year producing wonderfully structured and well-researched essays (yet another excuse for those who deliberately *don't* want to produce wonderfully structured and well-researched essays?).

If you have not produced essays of this nature during the year when time is at much less of a premium, you are certainly unlikely to start producing them in the exam. However, just in case you do have an incredible brainstorm, follow the rules on time allocation and you will be quite safe.

So the people really at risk are the hard workers (try not to laugh). Quick bit of chop logic to justify the Fraser laziness.

And, quite simply, it is not worth your while to produce such an answer in the exam. Although you have only an average of thirty-five minutes per question, as I have explained, most of the marks will appear in the first two-thirds of your answer. Of course it depends to some extent on the actual marking scheme being used by the Faculty, but as your answer proceeds the amount of marks available becomes much less. The points of law that require discussion will decrease, and the question may even contain one particular issue that requires specific knowledge of a recent case in order for the candidate to be able to answer that part of the question properly. Despite your incredible case learning technique, and all the law reports you have pored over, you may not know the actual case the examiner is after, and no amount of waffle will release those last three marks for you.

In fact, and this point gives engineers and mathematicians no end of amusement and merriment over their games of dungeons and dragons, it could be said that no-one is ever going to be awarded the full amount of marks for an answer in a law exam. If there is a total of 40 marks per question, then a mark of 35 or 36 is very good indeed. A mark of 37 is stratospherically good. You will never get the full 40.

So, if it were possible to produce a graph of time and effort taken, plotted against marks awarded, the gradient of the resulting curve would show that there is a flat end to the graph where, no matter how much time and effort you continue to put in, you will not get any more marks. [This paragraph is aimed at the engineers and mathematicians.]

You must make sure that you stop *way short* of this flat part of the graph. It is just not worth your time and trouble. This is why earlier in this chapter, when discussing the option of transferring a saved five-minute spell from one question to another, I said not to do it too much. Imagine you transfer a whole fifteen minutes from one question to another, because you feel you know one topic very well. Doubtless the question you transfer that fifteen minutes to *is* on a subject you know very well. Also, the question that the fifteen minutes is taken from is going to be on a topic at which you feel less than confident.

Yet you are now allowing yourself only twenty minutes for that question, and it is on a weak topic. You are automatically cutting down the amount of available marks. You will have fifty minutes on the other question, which is quite a long time. You will doubtless write away at top speed, in the fond belief that you are writing a really good answer. But how many marks are you gaining in those last fifteen minutes? Unless you write excessively long introductions, you will already have gained most of them in the first thirty-five minutes' worth of the answer.

And yet the question at which you do not think you are going to be any good, and on which you only spent twenty minutes, will have a great deal of very easy marks still available. Although you may not end up quite so pleased with the final product, the mathematical result (ie total marks for both the two questions) will almost certainly be higher if you forget your delusions of academic grandeur and do what you are supposed to do, namely spend only thirty-five minutes on each question. Force yourself to think harder about the weaker subject. You may surprise yourself and find out that, in fact, you do know a bit more about it than you initially thought.

(You may even find that you do not know quite so much about the other question, and may be struggling after half an hour to continue. You will then have to further transfer the spare twenty minutes on to another question, and so on. Do you see how ridiculous the whole thing can become?)

If you are still convinced that you know best, and you *can* create the perfect symphony on *Re Vandervell's Trusts (No 47)*, then only transfer an extra five minutes. It is not worth playing about any more than that to satisfy some stupid urge to do 'one really good question'.

EXTRA TIPS FOR THOSE AIMING FOR A FIRST

So that I cannot be accused of misrepresentation of any kind, I make these recommendations based on observation and research rather than a complete knowledge of what each establishment requires of the individual candidate before they will award this accolade.

One point before we start. If you aim for a First and fail, even by the merest shaving, then you have failed. Think no more about it – at least you tried.

OF COURSE, I WAS **THIS CLOSE** TO A FIRST

Above all, do not under any circumstances become one of those nauseous, unpleasant, whingeing individuals who, when asked about their degree, says 'I just missed a First'.

There are a lot of them about, which leads my suspicious mind to question the veracity of most of these people, but, apart from that, what makes them think that anybody wants to know? It is a matter solely for you, and aside from confessing your disappointment to your nearest and dearest at the time, forget about it. You know how close (or otherwise) it was, and that is the end of the matter.

When I meet people who say 'I just missed a First' I feel very sick, and swear obscenely at them until they take the hint and leave my company. It is pathetic indulgence and self-agrandissement, and have nothing to do with it.

And so on to technique for the Favoured First brigade. Of course a large amount of hints can also be found in the chapter on the different types of exam question (essay or problem) and you should study these carefully because the choice matters a little bit more to you than the vast majority of ordinary punters. You have to demonstrate to the examiner that you do, indeed, have the extra 'polish on the apple' necessary to achieve a First.

The Faculty will not hand these things out lightly, you know, because it really is a mark of true academic excellence. You will remember my little story earlier about the chap who, as an undergraduate, wrote his whole Roman Law examination paper in Latin. He is the sort of person who will be marking your paper. Frightening thought, isn't it? So you had better know your stuff if you are to attempt this, because if you try it and do *not* know your stuff, all that is waiting is major embarrassment all round.

In essay questions, as well as demonstrating a complete and thorough understanding of the legal principles and issues involved, discussion about policy or potential reforms always works like a charm. Of course, this policy must not be something you have just created yourself (there are few marks on the usual law exam marking plan for highly creative fiction) but sound and accurate. You will be given credit for this type of knowledge, and rightly so.

Equally with potential or pending reform. For example, if you happen to be aware of Green Papers (those Government documents so few people take any notice of) or Law Commission recommendations or reports, then include pertinent references to these things. This is, in my opinion, impressive scholarship (providing it is all relevant to the question itself) but then I have always been easily impressed. Remember to be relevant. It is no good discussing the proposed reforms to the law of family property for certain types of divorce settlement, when you are answering a question on the status of Marcus' slave after the chamber pot has hit him on the head (see above).

Also, another way to impress and do your cause untold good is to utilise knowledge that you may have picked up in one of your other subjects. For example, I was answering a question once on Human Rights in the European Community, with particular reference to the German Courts and the decision in *Wensch*. From one of my other courses, Civil Liberties, I happened to know something about that very subject in the Republic of Ireland. Lo and behold, I thought, the Republic of Ireland is a member of the European Community. [Well, in truth I had to think quite hard about whether it was or not, and in the end I took a gamble.]

So in went a paragraph on that, as a contrast to the German position. What scholarship, the examiner may have thought (certainly I was momentarily dazzled by my own brilliance), because it did the trick. Stay aware and a similar thing may well happen in your exams.

STRESS MANAGEMENT

This is the area of exams that probably troubles you the most. Certainly there are a great deal of people who worry, cannot sleep, lose their appetites, become ill, and generally behave as though they have a severe attack of food poisoning, simply because the exams are approaching.

One of the predominant causes of stress is that you, the candidate, believe that there is not sufficient time to prepare thoroughly and hence you believe you cannot do justice to the mighty intellect you fondly (and rather unjustifiably) hope nestles in your noggin. The ten-week plan should dispel that area of doubt and consequently release you from worries on that score. Still better, if you are reading this book *earlier* than a mere ten weeks before your first exam, then you really should be way ahead of the game and no worries about time should even cross your frontal lobe.

However, as you well know (particularly if you are a worrier) there is a whole smorgasbord of other worries to haunt you, even if the 'I don't have enough time! What shall I do? I DON'T HAVE ENOUGH TIME, I TELL YOU!!' worry has been laid to rest.

Here is a selection of the most common, together with suggested solutions thereto. I well know that worry is not always a rational thing, but maybe if you do actually consider the reasons behind your fears you will not get in such a state. So, onto the psychiatrist's couch with you.

And send me a hundred guineas for my trouble.

'I don't have enough time!'

Already dealt with above, just the very fact of reading this book should solve this particular concern. Even if you really *do not* have enough time, there is little for it but to buckle down and see how much you can manage in the time available. Certainly, warbling and wailing about it is not going to miraculously boost your chances, or transport you back in time to the beginning of the academic term. (Even if it could, you would probably still waste away the year and find yourself in this position, wouldn't you?)

'My mind just goes blank in exams'

This is often the result of anxiety, and what useful advice that is! Provided you have prepared sufficiently, you will have enough material to answer at least one question really well. Find your best question and answer that first. (Note: ensure you keep within your timing plan, however.) With luck, that will take your mind off your problem and all your secrets will be unlocked. If you really do go blank, how did you ever get to college? You must have written *something* before now. If it is really bad, seek professional help or hypnotism (my rates for both these things are really low) or change to a subject in which being blank in the exam is a positive advantage. Ever thought of Land Economy?

'I just can't face them!' (said hysterically)

Well, neither could I. This one just cannot be helped. Welcome to the real world. You will have to do lots of things you can't face.

Other miscellaneous problems

I once had to walk up and down outside the exam hall with a friend of mine to calm him down. It was just before a morning exam, and he was so stressed that he had *already* been sick twice (this was 9 am, and, before you ask, no, he hadn't been drinking heavily the night before). At one stage I did think that he was about to collapse.

In the end, a few deep breaths and a minute or two of cardio-pulmonary massage and he was right as rain.

This was the same individual who, three weeks before, was begging to take the exam then, because he knew it all and was ready to roll. Yes, he had peaked too early, and way too early at that. I doubt any of my readers will have that trouble, but bear it in mind. Timing is all important.

Another sad story to do with a lack of stress management was another friend who completely cracked up and was carted away. The writing was most definitely on the wall when, a few weeks before the exams, he became very upset that he was not allowed to study in the library *later than 10 pm!* Why he wanted to do this I do not know. He further objected to the noise in the (very quiet) library – you know, the sound of pages being turned, that sort of thing – to the extent that he would work in the furthest, quietest corner of the library *with his ears stuffed with cotton wool*. Of course, after six or seven weeks of this he couldn't cope any more (I'm amazed he lasted that long) and consequently went completely loopy. You will be happy to know that he is totally recovered now. The sad thing about him was that he knew so much more than even the people who took the paper and did well in it. He just became carried away by it all.

Make sure that this, too, does not happen to you.

So now you are even better prepared than you were at the end of Chapter 4. You now know how to deal with the difficulties of it all, as well as having super notes and a complete and thorough understanding of the case-law. The next problem area to tackle is that of which question to answer, and whether it is better for *you* individually to answer essay or problem questions, and the advantages and disadvantages of each. We will also look at some examples. So, on to Chapter 6 and forwards!

6
ESSAY AND PROBLEM TYPE QUESTIONS

This a further area in which the study and examination of law differs from most other subjects. Examinations in most of the other subjects in the Arts or Humanities (I've never understood what the 'Humanities' means either) simply require essays. Writing those essays may not, of course, be a particularly easy task to accomplish, and I dare say many of those successful in law exams would find it beyond them to tackle essays on some of those difficult history or English literature topics. However, you have to take and succeed in *law* exams and so the relative difficulties of other subjects is quite irrelevant.

If you have never before taken a law exam, and you do not quite understand the difference between an essay question and a problem question, then go and look at some past papers. Then come back to this page.

For those of you who have done it all before (and for those who have just arrived back breathless having looked at those past papers) let us consider the type of question which will suit our different types of candidate.

ESSAY QUESTIONS

Rather perversely, these questions suit both the very good and the very bad. Any one aiming for a First should definitely be attempting at least one (and probably two) because these questions are much harder to do well in. Thus if you are a very good candidate, you should be making the most of your advantages and showing the examiner just how good you really are (or think you are). A very good essay answer will generally obtain more credit than a very good problem answer, simply because the examiner is likely to see many more good problems than essays. (Of course, if you do five very good answers you should be on track anyway, regardless of the essay/problem ratio.)

The very bad may also find the essay question to their liking because it has a loose framework and a generality that allows the idiot candidate to waffle on for ever. As long as the idiot is somewhere in the region of the question matter, some marks can be had, whereas it is harder to do this (effectively steal marks from the examiner out of sympathy) in the more precise world of the problem.

PROBLEM QUESTIONS

These are best for all those in the middle of the range, ie those better than very bad, but not as accomplished as the very good. This almost certainly means *you*. Provided you have a modicum of analytic skills, the problem question will highlight the issues you must consider simply by the provision of information.

As an example, let's take the little story told in Chapter 5 about the thorny question of objects falling from windows in Ancient Rome. Now, you will remember that Marcus, the genial traveller, was struck, but so was his *slave*. You do not need to be a classical scholar to realise that (even if you do not know that there was a whole area of law regarding slaves) the fact that Marcus' slave was injured *must* give rise to a different set of considerations. If it did not, then why would the examiner have bothered putting all the extra details in, simply for you to repeat all the analysis contained in the section regarding Marcus? (As a further cautionary note, when at the end of a question you read the immortal line 'Would your answer to part (b) above be different if Shylock had been 19 years of age when he took the jewel-encrusted goblet from the dining room, rather than 22?' or something similar, it is a pretty safe bet that your answer to this slight change in the circumstances will *not* be: 'No, it would make no difference to my answer at all.' If you do think the answer is 'No', then think again, because nine times out of ten you will be wrong.)

We will now consider some examples of the genre, in the field of Family Law. I have chosen Family Law because the questions clearly do fall into one or other of the two categories. Also, I find Family Law problems amusing.

EXAMPLE 1

Question

'Co-habitants who terminate their relationship are in no worse a financial position vis-à-vis each other than had they been married. There is therefore no reason to legislate to expressly preserve a co-habitant's financial interest in property.' Discuss.

Comments and answer

Anyone who on reading this question does not automatically realise it is an essay question should consider a change of diet. Equally, anyone who is studying this subject who happens to agree with the postulation in the question is either a raving male chauvinist fascist or in need of a complete change of diet *and* surroundings.

The question is evidently a quotation, but whose quotation? This is usually the first point to consider in most essay questions. The questions will often contain quotations, and then a very terse instruction such as 'Discuss' or 'Consider'. The quotation will not usually be taken from any particular source, and hence usually you are not expected to recognise it. The examiner will usually make them up for the express purpose of using them in the exam paper. I created the above example for the express purpose of this chapter (hence why I am not an examiner).

You are *not* expected automatically to agree with any such postulation, and in some cases the quotation may be so extreme that the examiner will be astounded if anyone actually does agree with it. Do not be afraid to disagree with any of these hypotheses, regardless of whether or not you think they are extreme. You will not be marked on your point of view (unless I am marking the paper, and that is highly unlikely) and the examiner is obviously merely starting from a point whereby you can argue and discuss; in a way, playing the Devil's Advocate. However, there will be the odd essay question which will use as a quotation a famous passage from a famous judgment, or other worthy text. An example would be Lord Atkin's neighbour principle, from *Donoghue* v *Stevenson*.

There may be only a mark or two for the art of 'name that quotation', but if no source is given and you are unfamiliar with *both* the subject and whence it came I would not attempt the question. Move on to another question, after having ascertained that you are in the correct exam hall. You may have gone into the history exam by mistake. If you cannot name the source, but can answer the question, then go ahead and do so.

And so on to the answer itself. *I must emphasise that this is not a suggested solution.* Rather, I will discuss it generally and highlight the points that should be contained in your answer. The principle in the question is, in my opinion, quite incorrect. In fact, I would be surprised if there were any tutors in the subject who would agree with the proposition that *no* legislation is needed. This is because there is a dichotomy between changing social values and the law that provides for what happens when a close relationship breaks down.

For all you dummies who are not aware of it, 'co-habitants' (within the scope of this question; strictly speaking, as you know, anyone who lives with someone else *co-habits* with them) refers to unmarried couples. Sometimes this is also called being a common-law husband and wife. The term may also include the sort of arrangement whereby a man maintains a mistress (very Parisian, though she may not live in Paris. Penge, more probably.)

One of the cases in this area is *Horrocks* v *Foray*, which is about a man who maintained a mistress and provided accommodation for her for 17 years. Thus even if you took the view that the question was really only concerned with the common-law husband/wife situation, it would do no harm to mention this area briefly.

Incidentally, in *Horrocks* v *Foray*, the Court refused to apply the contractual licence argument, deciding that the man had provided accommodation for his mistress and her child out of generosity, not because of a binding obligation. This provides a somewhat interesting perspective to the 'maintained mistress' scenario. Generosity, indeed. I wonder if the individual in question then decided, purely out of generosity of course, to maintain another mistress who was 17 or so years younger?

So, firstly, you have to define what you mean by 'co-habitee' and/or what you take the question to mean by 'co-habitee'. If you are going to discuss the requirements for 'co-habitee' status, is the existence of a sexual relationship sufficient or is more required? All this has to be covered, and you will be accumulating marks as you go.

The predominant part of the question obviously requires a comparison between the rules governing the break-up of a marriage and those applied when co-habitees suffer a similar relationship crisis. The former is governed by statute, and you should identify the statutes and refer to the relevant provisions, and the latter is governed by the orthodox principles of property law and trusts.

Thus, if you are also taking exams in Land Law or Equity, you may have some of that 'cross-knowledge' I mentioned in the previous chapter. For example, the sort of basic knowledge of constructive trusts that would be bread-and-butter stuff in the Land Law exam could get you a large amount of extra credit in this Family Law answer.

One good way of ensuring that you produce a structured and properly thought-out answer is to prepare a brief plan on rough or spare paper before you start. Include the names of all the cases you wish to refer to, and put an asterix or other mark by the really important ones (here, cases such as *Burns* v *Burns*, *Grant* v *Edwards*, *Pettitt* v *Pettitt*). These will also form part of the plan; for example, write a paragraph on *Burns* v *Burns* and so on.

Of course, keep an eye both on the time and the plan to ascertain your progress and the amount you still have to do. Remember, only thirty-five minutes (if the paper requires five questions) and that time will *soon* pass. In a way, the better prepared you are, the more ruthless you have to be regarding what to leave out, because you will have a surfeit of knowledge. The duffers who can barely remember what co-habitee means will have dried up after fifteen minutes.

And, finally, if the question asks for a decision from you, then provide one. For example, in this question if, instead of 'Discuss', the question had asked 'Do you agree with this?' then jolly well make sure you say if you do or not. No-one likes a wishy-washy answer – John Major is not marking your script.

EXAMPLE 2

Question (Note: if you think this question is long, wait until you see your exam paper. You're in for a fright.)

François is a professional footballer from Marseilles, sent for a three-week trial with Melchester Rovers in June 1988. The manager of Melchester, Kenny le Scot, told François that he would like him to join the club full-time, but Melchester already had the maximum two foreign players permitted by the League, Tito and Toto the dazzling Yugoslavian midfield duo. François, a free spirit who despises agents and lawyers (and unaware of the existence of the European Community) decided that the only solution was to acquire British residency. Accordingly, he attempted to persuade Katrine, the club physiotherapist who had treated his recent hamstring trouble, to go through a ceremony of marriage with him. Aware of the difference François would make to Melchester's strike force, she did go through such a ceremony with him in August 1988 (in time for pre-season training.)

Almost immediately, François was chosen for the first team by Kenny, where his goal-scoring prowess complemented the tactical brilliance of Tito and Toto. Katrine, desperate for love and affection, frequently asked François both (a) to move into her flat and (b) to consummate their marriage, but he refused to do either, on the grounds that (a) his flat was much closer to the football ground, and (b) his football would suffer.

In fact, he was secretly having an affair with Nicole who worked in 'Le Croissant Shop' in Melchester, and Nicole would stay in his flat overnight about two or three times a week.

Katrine began to get very lonely, and had a one-night stand with Georgio, a visiting European TV football commentator also from Marseilles who had come to see François play. She had a child by Georgio in September 1989, whom she christened Harry. By now François was a big star at Melchester, which prides itself on being a family club, and to avoid a scandal it was agreed that François and Katrine would bring up Harry; Georgio could visit him whenever he came to England.

Melchester have just won the FA Cup 1–0, the one goal coming from a controversial penalty awarded five minutes from time when François was 'brought down in the box'. Katrine and François have fallen out because she is convinced that François was not tripped, as he claims, but misled the referee.

'That was never a penalty. Give him an Oscar. Rovers' good name is ruined for ever. Now I know why the French don't play cricket – they haven't got a clue about good sportsmanship. I never want to see that no-good Frenchman again, and he can stay away from Harry,' she has been quoted as saying.

François and Nicole have now confessed all to Katrine and are living together openly. They want to bring up Harry. Kenny le Scot has proposed to Katrine.

Advise Katrine generally.

Comments and answer

That this is a long and daunting problem question there can be no doubt. Many problem questions appear at first sight to be dreadfully convoluted and complicated. However, in my opinion, the longer a question is in terms of text, the easier it is likely to be. This is because the issues are there to be picked out, and in a way the question itself acts as a sort of plan taking you from issue to issue.

Do not be one of those people who are frightened off long problem questions, because they are a rich source of exam marks. Also, your analysis will gain you credit even if you cannot recall (or perhaps you never knew) the precise case or statutory provision that goes with each of the issues.

Do not be afraid of posing another question in your answer itself. Half the skill of being a lawyer is knowing what questions to ask, as my Director of Studies used to say. If you cannot decide a particular point on the strength of the information in the question, then say so and you will get credit for it.

Do *not* under any circumstances 'identify the issues' in your first paragraph exhaustively, reciting a list parrot-fashion. It wastes time and will gain you no marks. In a long question like this, it may take you up to twenty minutes. Do not waste time in this way. If you *must* 'identify the issues' because it relaxes you or helps you to think clearly, then do so *very briefly*. For example:

> Katrine's problems fall into one of these two broad categories: the status of her marriage and the status of the child, and the remedies available to her in respect of each.

I do not pretend that this is an ideal or perfect way to start, and it could certainly be improved upon. However, it is broadly correct and will allow your answer to proceed in a certain way.

Note that you are asked to advise Katrine, so *please* advise her. There is no need to sit on the fence where you are asked to do something from her point of view.

As an illustration, if you decide to hypothesise about the François/Nicole attempt to gain custody of Harry, do so as a contingency Katrine must face, rather than 'If François really wants to bring up Harry he should be told that he will have to make an application under section ... etc etc.' It may amount to the same content in the end, but you will get more marks for style the first way than the second. This is all common sense, but so few of us have it and it often deserts us in the heat of the exam.

Again, and this is *very* important, there may very well be the odd red herring in the question, and you should realise that and be wary. Whether you just ignore the red herring altogether, or whether you actually state 'Katrine need not concern herself with ... at this stage because it is irrelevant to the question of ....' depends on the amount of time available to you. Do not under any circumstances be drawn into discussion regarding the red herrings.

There are quite a few red herrings in the question. I should know, I put them in deliberately.

List of red herrings in the question

(This is a Family Law paper, remember.)

a) Any league rules regarding the maximum number of foreign players per team.

b) Any Community legislation regarding free trade and cross-border movement of workers, 1992 and all that.

c) François' dislike of agents and lawyers (who can blame him?).

d) Any discussion about acquiring British residency.

e) Katrine's reasons, understandable though they may be, for the one-night stand with Georgio. (This may be one that is worth expressly discounting, thus showing that you are a sympathetic, human, caring candidate as well as a damned fine lawyer.)

f) Tito and Toto and their undoubtedly superb, one might say intuitive, reading of the offside trap, Brian.

You will, however, have to know your stuff in order to be capable of deciding what is, and what is not, a red herring. Here, then, are some of the issues.

1) Is the marriage of Katrine and François valid?
2) If not, why not?
3) If it is, what can be done about it now?
4) What are the grounds for annulment?
5) What are the grounds for divorce?
6) Which apply, or may apply, in this case and why?
7) Was François justified in putting his football before his wife's wishes, and the legal requirement for consummation?
8) If he may have been, of what relevance is his dalliance with Nicole?
9) Is the initial secrecy of the François/Nicole affair of any relevance whatsoever?
10) What is the status of poor little Harry, the tug-of-love child?
11) What has Georgio, the natural father, to do with it?
12) Does it matter if Harry has been treated as a child of the family, and by whom?
13) Has he?
14) Of what relevance are the supposed morals of Melchester Rovers?*
15) What is Kenny le Scot's golf handicap? (Oh, sorry, that should have been in the red herring column.)
16) Of what relevance is the argument between Katrine and François regarding his dubious continental Wembley tactics?*
17) Of what relevance is Katrine's possible marriage to Kenny le Scot?
18) What are Melchester's chances in the League next season? (Whoops, there I go again.)

*To the unwary and untutored, these two may have appeared as red herrings. Of course they are not.

(14) is relevant and warrants discussion regarding whether Harry has been treated as a child of the family by François, or was it a sham designed to fool the readers of *Roy of the Rovers* magazine, with François in reality having little to do with Harrykins at all?

(16) is relevant regarding irretrievable breakdown of marriage and whether Katrine finds it intolerable to live with François.

Now, I do not propose to give you a suggested or model solution to the question. Needless to say, there are innumerable cases and statutes that you will have to provide in your answer to gain full marks.

However, imagine for a moment that you do *not* know any of the relevant cases or statutes. Imagine that you have answered four out of the necessary five questions, you have ignored my advice and blown your timing and you have only fifteen minutes left. (This will also be covered in a later chapter on Damage Limitation.) I hope that you are able to see that, even in such dire circumstances, there are marks to be had from a problem question, even if all you do is go through the question, identifying the issues and giving brief conclusions. This is so, even if you do so only in note form. Bear it in mind.

One word of warning. Because the examiners are quite bright, and generally interesting individuals, some problem questions may actually be amusing or otherwise interesting little pieces of fiction. Do not be so interested in the story itself that you forget you are in an exam and write a correspondingly witty little playlet in response. You will gain no credit for it. You are in there for serious academic stuff, and don't you forget it.

EXAMPLE 3

Question

'The Guardianship of Minors Act lays down, as a foundation, the welfare of the child as the paramount consideration.' Is this a correct statement of the law? What improvements would you make to the Act?

Comments and answer

This is an ideal example of the rule of law exams, 'The shorter the question, the harder the answer.' I hope that you can see that this is a very difficult question. Even if you happen to be a very good candidate (dream on) this would be a real nightmare to answer well.

When you compare it to the great François question, it really does show why you should welcome problem questions with open arms. This question gives you nothing whatsoever around which to construct your answer.

The only slight point in favour of the foolish is the first part of the question, which asks if the hypothesis is correct. This will allow you, briefly, to cover a little ground and attempt to quickly harvest any marks that may be going for that section. This will not take you very long, as you should realise that there will not be that much reward for a detailed and philosophical analysis of what the examiner means by 'foundation'. You are not in a competition to win a job publishing a dictionary; you are in a law exam and you will suddenly find yourself with twenty-five of your thirty-five minutes left to discuss any reforms you think necessary to an Act of Parliament.

The problem is that such questions require a sweeping and broad knowledge, of a kind very few candidates possess. If you are forced to answer such a question without being fully happy about it, for example because it is compulsory or it is the best available as your last question, you can attempt to broaden it slightly without being too diverse.

For example, you can bring in the other statutes that have the requirement of welfare as a paramount consideration. This of course presupposes a familiarity with such statutes – the last thing you want to be doing is trawling through your statute book, looking for the pithy phrase 'welfare as paramount consideration' or words similar.

You can also discuss what the phrase 'paramount consideration' actually means, and I seem to remember that such an argument flourished briefly in the Family Division before a robust judge put an end to all that 'shilly shallying'.

'It means what it says – paramount means paramount. Plain English. Don't know what all the fuss is about' etc etc. So, sadly, not much mileage there.

But, no matter how much you may wriggle and fight like a strong fish caught on a hook, in the end you are going to have to address yourself to that thorny question –reform of the Act.

Earlier I mentioned Green Papers and legislative reform as a way of impressing the Faculty and, perhaps, demonstrating the polish and maybe getting a First. That is all very well if it is voluntary, and put in an answer to show a complete and very academic grasp of that topic. Even a good candidate, faced with a positive *requirement* to discuss reform, may find it difficult. Consider for a moment. Practically the *whole question* is about reform of the Act.

You may not be aware of any pending changes. That will become glaringly obvious to whoever has the delightful task of marking your paper, and you will gain little credit from your ignorance. You may be aware of a Green Paper or recommendations of a Commission or suchlike, but without specific knowledge of any proposals and an ability to refer to these you will not do very well.

The bottom line is, if you are forced by circumstance to do an essay question that is very short like this and requires much concrete knowledge (rather than 50 per cent waffle you can sometimes get away with) then you may well be doomed. Far better to do a problem question instead, even if you happen to hate football.

EXAMPLE 4

Question

Terence and Emma were married in 1988. Terence's father, Fred, a wealthy businessman, bought a house for the couple to live in, and put it in Terence's name. The house, 'Lusty Glade', is in Yorkshire where Fred lives and where Terence and Emma plan to live. He gave them the keys the day they returned from honeymoon, saying 'When I got married your mother and I lived in a little one-room flat for nearly two years. Nothing like that is going to happen to either of you if I can help it.'

Emma is not employed, spending her time looking after their child Jimmy and decorating 'Lusty Glade' to a very high standard. Word of the interior has spread, and *Home and Hearth*, the well known interior design magazine, has just featured it in the May issue. Emma has consequently been offered a highly-paid job completely re-designing the interior of a top London hotel.

Emma's relationship with Terence has consequently broken down. Terence has said 'No wife of mine has to work. Why does she want a job? We don't need the money. She'll be earning more than me! That can't be right. Besides, if Jimmy grows up with those soft Southerners he'll never be good enough to fulfil his destiny as opening batsman for Yorkshire and full-back for Leeds Rugby League Club.'

Emma now wants to know what her financial position will be if she divorces Terence and moves to London. Advise her.

Assume that the parties have agreed that Terence can have custody of Jimmy, providing Emma can see her son one weekend every month and for two weeks each summer.

Comments and answer

This is obviously not such a long question as the first problem question about the Melchester Rovers saga. Also, a great deal of the substance of the problem at first glance, namely custody of the child, is removed by the last couple of lines stating the agreed custody arrangements.

However, you must always read problem questions *very carefully indeed*, and this is no exception. This is because the question may contain the odd little hint or piece of further information that will suggest what areas of the law you should be considering and including in your answer. Read the question again, and write out a list of the issues in the same manner I did for Melchester Rovers. (Remember *never* do this in an exam itself, it is a waste of time.)

Try to see if you have missed any out. I will produce my own list a little further on, but one issue which is fairly well hidden and you may have missed is the new relative earning power of Emma and Terence.

Terence complains that Emma will now be earning more than him. Whilst this is put in along with a great deal of irrelevant information (Terence's hopes for his son's sporting career holding little appeal for the exam marking plan), it does raise the possibility of financial provision from one spouse to the other. Stereotypes being what they are, you can be assured a great many candidates would have missed this. They will have looked at the position of Emma, and assessed whether Terence should pay any money to Emma. Few of them will have considered the converse position, namely whether Emma will have to pay anything to Terence and/or Jimmy.

Do not be caught out this way yourself. Whether you pride yourself on your modern attitude or revel in your misogyny, examine each aspect of each question in a completely objective way.

Other issues include:

a) The ownership of the house in such situations generally.

b) The ownership of the house, taking into account the circumstances in which Terence and Emma came into possession of it.

c) Fred's form of words (partly included in (b) above, and a good chance to cross-reference any information you may have from Land Law).

d) The value Emma's decorations will have regarding an assessment of any interest she may have.

e) The relevance of apportionment of fault in the breakdown of a relationship.

f) Whether Emma will be able to obtain a divorce on the facts contained in the question, and, if not, what other factors need to be present.

So evidently less complex than Melchester Rovers, but you will obviously have to examine each issue in substantially more detail as a consequence.

So you can see that there are a number of major differences in approach between the two different types of question that you will be faced with. You should be sufficiently aware of your own abilities (and lack thereof) in the different areas to realise which of the two you are best at.

One final point. Never *learn* essays themselves so that, in the (unlikely) event of that precise question actually being included in the exam paper, you can simply regurgitate the already prepared answer. It is a waste of time because you are much better served by having the facts and law at your fingertips and producing what is relevant to fit any particular question. This applies *particularly* to essays or articles that are not your own. The examiner will be able to spot plagiarism a mile off, and give you little credit therefor.

7
FINE TUNING

Before you read this chapter, you are allowed to have a cup of coffee (or herbal tea, if you insist) and take a deep breath. Sigh with relief for a moment or two. Take another deep breath. Aaah. Look out of the window and marvel at the puppies gambolling on the freshly cut lawn – I know, you don't feel that you should, but there is a reason for this heresy. All will be revealed.

The reason that I am advocating such a departure from my hitherto strict rules of exam preparation behaviour is simple. By the time you reach this chapter, you should have accomplished about 80 per cent of the hard work. Of course, this is not to say that you can relax, have *two* cups of coffee or watch the puppies gambolling for longer than five or ten minutes, oh no. The remaining 20 per cent is tremendously important. However, the work that you should have done already will have laid a solid foundation for your forthcoming success and so you are entitled to feel pleased with yourself for a little while.

[Note: if you have reached this chapter and you *have not* yet accomplished all that you are supposed to have done, then there are two alternatives. Firstly, you have been very clever and are reading ahead. Far from it being mid-May, it is still November, and you are months ahead of the game. If you fall into this category, then you are forgiven your lack of a complete set of notes. If, however, it is *not* November, but rather it is mid-May (or even later!), your exams are fast approaching and you have not compiled the necessary materials, then (a) you have blown it, and (b) you had better have a good excuse ready for all those people you will disappoint once the results come out.]

Now, stop day dreaming and back to reality. This chapter is the equivalent of the coach's pep-talk before the big game, the Formula 1 mechanic adjusting the spark-plugs or the concert violinists playing those bizarre notes five minutes before the conductor walks out. You need to come to terms with the following fact of life.

Regardless of how much (or how little) you have done prior to walking into that exam hall, your performance in those three hours will make (or break) your academic pretensions in that subject. This is, of course, absolutely obvious – a simple truth, you may think, and hence often overlooked.

Thus, and I make no apology for repeating advice already given earlier in the book, you can go into that exam on Land Law not really knowing the difference between a mortgage and a lease, but if you manage to fluke five questions on all the other topics you can still emerge triumphant. Equally, you may be so strong in the subject that you have been holding private seminars at the Faculty, but if you blow it in there all the world will take you as a fraud.

The important thing about taking all this advice is not to let it stress you out. Think too hard about the disadvantages of the exam system and you will begin to feel undue pressure and may very well end up feeling so wound up you are tempted to throw in the towel, go to Brighton and get a job as a deck-chair attendant. Resist such dark thoughts. Make the system work *for* you, not against you. That is why you have paid ten gold pieces for this scholarly work. (Well, part-scholarly work.)

Stress has many different effects on many different people. There are those who thrive on it – some athletes, for example, need it in order to perform well, and would not be able to achieve their best time, distance or whatever without it. However, others find that stress makes them feel ill, helpless or weak (or even all three) and it is these people whose performance is most likely to suffer from an excess of stress.

You will know which of the two broad categories you fall into, and whether or not stress is likely to help or hinder you. Certainly if you are one of those lucky people who *do* thrive on stress there is little that I can usefully advise you regarding stress management or other home-spun philosophy to help you get through the nerves of it all.

However, you are probably one of the terrified crowd, so you should start considering ways in which you can reduce the sometimes drastic effects of being stressed out of your skull.

I advocate the following simple steps, which some of you may find absurd in their simplicity, to minimise the amount of trauma that you will face during your exam period. You will have enough on your plate without worrying about, or otherwise concerning yourself with, the sort of complications that these simple points are designed to avoid.

a) Ensure that you do not leave yourself *anything whatsoever* that needs to be done on the day of the exam itself. This applies no matter whether the exam is in the morning or the afternoon, and applies equally to reading notes, looking at cases, buying extra pens or cartridges, or anything else. Of course, this does not mean that you are not allowed to read notes, look at cases etc on the day of an exam. On the contrary, and particularly if you have an afternoon paper, I hope that you will take the opportunity to spend some time going over various details of an academic nature. The point is that you should not leave things undone in the days immediately before, so that you *have* to read a certain chapter or look up a particular series of cases on the day itself. It will just give you one extra thing to do, and hence increase the pressure on your time (and hence your potential stress levels).

b) Know *exactly* where the exam is being held, and how you are going to get there.

If you are particularly susceptible to panic, you can even go to the lengths of tracing and timing your route so that you know at what time precisely you should leave etc. Cynics may mock at this, but even something as simple as knowing where the heck you are supposed to be can be overlooked, so great is your concern at deciphering the intricacies of constructive trusts.

c)   Know the procedure for the exam itself. Of course you should long ago have worked out exactly how many questions you have to answer and so on, but your particular university, polytechnic or college may have pecadilloes of its own. For example, the institution where I took my degree had an amusing little variation on the theme of actually starting the paper. Remember all the exams that you took at school, 'A' Levels and so forth? Well, you probably all filed into the exam hall about five or ten minutes before the exam was to start, and perhaps the invigilator gave all of you some instructions and maybe a little piece of advice or two. The exam paper itself may have been on your desk already, or would have been handed out (face down) shortly after you all arrived. Then, at about ten seconds before the exam was to start, he or she would kindly announce 'You may now start.' You would then be off like the field in the Grand National.

You may fondly imagine it is the same in higher education. Not where I was it wasn't, oh no. Where I was, the procedure went a little like this. We would all arrive at the exam hall, and wait for the doors to open. It would usually be raining. Of course, I would never have an umbrella with me, and so I would get wet and nurse feelings of revenge about those who *did* have an umbrella. Not that the weather is relevant to the story, of course, but I like to give you a little flavour and background. Anyway, the doors would open about ten minutes before the exam was due to start, and we would all file in.

And this is where the amusement would set in. For anyone who adopted the school exam technique of sitting and waiting to be told they were allowed to start would still have been sitting there three hours later when they would be told to stop writing.

No instructions were ever given. Nothing would be said by the invigilators that would lead anybody to conclude that they were permitted to start sharing their knowledge. Everyone was just expected to know.

Of course, this had some splendid results. Realisation would gradually dawn on the hapless candidates who had not been forewarned about these peculiarities of exam technique. This delay would cost them at least ten minutes, and some less than hardy souls (who would not feel comfortable about ordering a coffee in a café on their own initiative) would often last for as much as twenty minutes before the penny finally dropped and they managed to summon up enough courage to pick up their pen and start. (If I appear somewhat scornful of these wimps, it is because I am. What did they think would happen to them if they started? That they would be thrown out of the exam, along with the other 50 people all doing the same thing?)

d) Ensure that you get enough sleep for four or five nights, at least, before your first paper. In fact, you should have been diligent throughout your whole revision period about getting enough sleep. It is not quite so darkly romantic and somewhat gothic as staying up all night, but it is much more sensible. If you *are* romantically inclined, you can always lie afterwards and tell exotic, mysterious and highly untrue accounts about your sleep patterns. (This applies equally to eating and taking exercise – mens sana in corpore sano, and all that. I have done my best not to bore you with personal advice about how to run your life.)

The reason that I encourage you to get enough sleep is because of another story about someone else, who before his exam in Roman Law stayed up all night in order to make sure that he was fully up-to-date on such a living, changing subject. This was extremely foolish, as he discovered in the exam itself when, exhausted by his overnight vigil, he fell asleep, being woken up in a kindly fashion by the invigilator after a refreshing kip of about forty minutes. Take note and do not make the same mistake as he did. (I will not tell you what class he obtained in that paper out of a sense of professional delicacy.)

It is easy to give advice, I know, but do try not to worry. There is nothing to worry about, after all. The odd dreadful story of exam candidates having breakdowns, and worse, are really very sad. Try to keep a sense of proportion about the whole fiasco.

And so on to fine tuning itself. What should you be doing in the last couple of weeks?

SHORT NOTES

There are those who use these extensively, and it is certainly true that if you *have* actually taken the effort to compile very full, admirable notes (as I'm sure you will have done) then these will be too full and lengthy to use in the last couple of weeks, which is the time that you should be actually *learning* the fine detail. Short notes comprise all the essential points written in truncated form, so that they can actually be used as a revision aid.

Some idiots think they are compiling short notes by simply writing their notes out again, only in a very small writing, thus ending up with fewer pages. As usual, not only are they deluding themselves and demonstrating a complete inability to grasp even the rudimentary basics of selection, but with any luck they may get cramp from writing such tiny characters.

Further, do not be disheartened that you have to recommence writing out notes of one sort or another. After all, and particularly those of you on the Ten Week Special plan, you will have only recently finished compiling your proper notes themselves.

There are two points worth making here. The first one is that, if you *do* want to make short notes, make sure that doing so does not use up so much of your time that other essential steps are not taken (such as the work needed on all those cases you have not heard of). The second point is that, bothersome though it is, all this note-taking, analysis of your notes, refining what is contained and what is not etc will have the beneficial effect that your knowledge will (perhaps subconsciously) increase.

I don't mind if you roundly curse me regularly for my badgering about making notes, reading cases, then preparing short notes etc, and for all the other boring tasks that I have set you, if, by doing them, you suddenly realise that in fact you have accumulated some knowledge almost as a side-effect of completing those tasks.

If you do make short notes, still read your full notes from time to time. This will help to keep your interest, because as you know variety is the spice of life, and it will also give you a wider framework within which to place your extremely specialised knowledge (which is what you will get by revising from short notes for extended periods).

Also, you must not be too narrow-minded to alter completely your strategy on one or two topics if it appears to you that you are on the wrong track entirely or you have missed out something essential. Now this is a very tricky area, and you must be well aware of the somewhat pathetic attitude adopted by some law students to prevent other candidates doing well. I briefly alluded to it when I was discussing borrowing other people's notes. There are those who deliberately attempt to mislead their brethren. We will look at one-up-manship in a more light-hearted way in the next chapter, but if you come across a couple of colleagues discussing a case you have never heard of in hushed tones of awe, then you may have missed it out completely or you may be the victim of a hoax.

I will leave it up to you to decide how to discern what the true situation is, but if the likelihood is that you *have* missed something out, or are unaware of a fairly major development, then do not stand on your dignity and decline to follow up the line of inquiry.

As another example of not becoming set in your ways, do make sure that you read the law reports in the serious daily newspapers over the last couple of weeks before the exam. This is not because anything relevant will come up – it will probably not. Even if a relevant case does happen to appear in the day or two before the exam, you will not be penalised if you do not mention it. However, there *is* credit to be had for keeping your eyes open and writing an exam question that is bang up to date.

THE FINAL HOURS

Your behaviour in the last few hours before the exam depends upon whether or not the exam is in the morning or the afternoon. Your timetable, drawn up all those chapters ago, will (if you did it properly) have taken account of the frequency of your exams and how much time you have between each.

If you have an exam in the afternoon, then of course you should do your best to make the most of those useful morning hours to tune in and turn on all that knowledge. (If you have a morning exam and an afternoon exam on the same day, then tough luck. You are going to be somewhat drained at the end of that little nightmare.) So you are allowed to read your notes and check your cases etc. But, remember, do not leave yourself anything that you *have* to do in that time. This will only increase your stress levels.

If, however, the exam in question is in the morning, then a completely different set of rules applies. You should not look at your notes at all. Not one little peep. You should get to bed early the night before (none of this nocturnal rubbish, remember), rise nice and early and eat a hearty breakfast, whether you feel like eating or not. Set off in good time, have a good laugh when you see a potential screamer walk into a lamp-post, and then stay well away from the fools outside the exam hall 'testing' each other. You are not interested in either their opinions or their inability to cope with their nerves, so do not encourage them.

One further point. There is a depressing number of people who, after coming out of an exam, cannot resist discussing their paltry attempts at various questions, and given half a chance these dullards will prattle on ad nauseam, telling each other everything about the last three hours of their life. Have no truck with this either. Once you put your pen down and leave the exam hall, there is nothing you can do to improve your performance and quite frankly it can only demolish your confidence to find out that you have missed something essential. Don't bother to talk to them. Save yourself from the boredom. If you *want* to be bored for twenty minutes, go and read the phone book.

DAMAGE LIMITATION

This is all extremely simple, and doubtless many of you will find no useful advice here. In fact, some of you may be so upset at the elementary nature of much that I have to say that it would be best for you to miss this section out altogether.

There are those cynics who take the view that the entire exam is one big exercise in damage limitation. Another way of putting it is that throughout your answers you are not so much demonstrating what you know, rather you are attempting to disguise the (often vast) gaps in your knowledge. I do not propose to be drawn into philosophical discussions of this nature. Besides, I know nothing about gaps in knowledge because there were never any gaps in mine (and if you believe that you'll believe anything).

However, regardless of the accuracy or otherwise of such hypothesising, there is a lot of truth in that school of thought regarding covering up gaps and damage limitation. Certainly, if you consider that you may be asked to answer five questions out of a total of only eight or ten, then you could find yourself in real difficulties depending on how complete the coverage is of topics.

It is this coverage, sometimes very narrow, that leads to an exam being thought 'hard' or 'easy'. Consider a hypothetical paper on, say, the Law of Tort. The exam with wide coverage may ask questions about a whole range of topics.

Something for everyone, in a way, and because there will only be one or two questions on, say, Negligence, then the questions will be much more general and hence easier to answer to an average standard. (Of course, damage limitation is all about getting up to that average standard, Anyone attempting to do *well* at the exam will not be so happy at an exam paper with very general coverage because he or she will have less opportunity to show off.)

However, the harder exam will perhaps have seven or eight of the questions on an area such as Negligence, and completely omit the odd topic that everyone would know at least something about (for example *Rylands* v *Fletcher*). Worse still, the number of questions about Negligence will mean that each of them requires knowledge on a very specialised area.

The available marks for waffling in an average way (to get marks of an average number) will be very few. Hence those of you who are not on the ball will need to limit the damage.

Let us assume that there are ten available questions, and you have to answer five. You look at the paper. It is very narrow coverage and your heart sinks. All those topics on which you could write a thesis do not appear. You feel your pulse race and your bowels turn to water. Oh dear. Never fear, you can now exercise your new-found technique on damage limitation.

The overriding rule is to hold your nerve. You must not panic under any circumstances. Panic will finish you off. Some people panic easily, others less so. If you have never taken a law exam in Higher Education before, you may not know if you are likely to panic or not. My advice is, be aware of the possibility that you may panic. Do *not* ignore the possibility because you think you are something of an ice-man or ice-woman because it will catch you unprepared, and you then have to deal not only with the damage to your legal career but also the damage to the psyche caused by realising that you are not as cool as you thought. So, take a couple of deep breaths and do not panic. Count up to ten or something, but keep a rein on your trauma.

The first thing to do is decide which questions you cannot attempt *at all*. If you are panicking, you may decide that you cannot do any of the ten at all, and want to leave the room. It is this that causes some people to become what I term 'screamers'.

Of course, not all of them do actually scream. But some of them do, and very amusing it is too. These are the people for whom it all becomes too much. Research shows that these people are more likely to have adopted the working pattern that early in this book I warned you not to adopt, namely the nocturnal vigil. This is often compounded by doing bizarre things like:

a) pasting notes to the ceiling of one's bedroom so one can read them for those few hours whilst in bed (this demonstrates a sad lack of imagination, and upside-down priorities, as well as a paucity of very close friends);

b) wearing ear plugs in the very quietest library so that one is not disturbed by the sound of one's own heart beating in an irritatingly loud fashion;

c) not eating because one does not have enough time;

d) reading short notes (often merely the same as one's ordinary notes only in very tiny writing so one suffers eye strain) at any available moment. This becomes particularly amusing when done whilst walking along the street, because it often results in collisions with those rapidly swerving objects, namely lamp-posts and letter-boxes.

You can tell that avoidance of most of the above would give you a generally better and healthier life-style, but I will refrain from giving you further advice about diet, exercise etc.

Back to the screamers. They look at the first question or two, decide they cannot answer them, and begin to panic. A little later (they may even begin to write out an answer) they can be observed desperately leafing through the entire paper, scouring it for even an inkling of a question that they can recognise.

Of course, they fail to discover such a nugget, and even if they did they would not recognise it because by then they are sweating, worrying, losing their grip on reality and descending into temporary madness. They leave the room shortly afterwards, often screaming.

Where do they go? How long does it take them to recover? Why are they in such a hurry? Do they have another pressing appointment (at the tea shop, perhaps)?

All these questions and more puzzle me, but I have never followed a screamer to find out the answers.

Needless to say, I do not expect or encourage you to find out the answers for me, either. Of course, the thing that the screamers do not realise is that, no matter what they do in the two or so hours unexpectedly available to them, it cannot do anything whatsoever towards helping them to pass that exam. For as long as you are sitting in that exam hall, pen in hand and brain in gear (even if it is only in first gear), you are progressing towards helping the examiner give you marks.

So, back to damage limitation. Decide which ones you definitely *cannot* attempt. If there are five of them, then your choice is made for you. If less than five, then what is the big problem? What are you worrying about the paper for? Choose your best five and get going.

If there are *more* than five that you cannot do, you are in a little difficulty. The best thing to do is to choose one you can do, and the one available that you feel best about (or think that you can attempt most strongly, to use exam-speak). This is because you want to start as strongly as you can, because the momentum that you may build up can often pull you through another question or two. Basic advice I know, but work your way through those that you can at least attempt, keeping to your time constraints, and doing your best. We will now end up with your having answered three, say, with two more to do and nothing left that you know the faintest thing about on the paper.

Obviously, again, you have to answer the full five questions, so what do you do? Which ones do you do?

Well, you avoid those very short essay questions. Much too difficult, as we discussed earlier in the book. You can either do the very long problem questions, and simply analyse them, discussing issues etc. I once did this, and very amusing it was too. (Probably not for the poor examiner who had to mark it, though.) Use of this technique will permit the examiner to award you at least a few marks out of his bag of goodies. More marks than you would get if you were in the tea shop, at any rate.

Alternatively you can answer, or attempt to answer, the longer (and hence slightly easier) essay questions. The trick here is to attempt those that allow you to draw on your general knowledge. Tackle the question as though you were answering a competition essay, using all the arguments and analytical skill at your disposal. You may have views on the subject from what you have read in newspapers or heard on the radio, for example. Whatever you do, you provide as much material as you can which is concerned (even obliquely) with the question, so that the examiner can award you some marks. Damage limitation. You want *something* out of that marking plan, even if it's just a mark for writing neatly.

The final technique, and somewhat controversial it is too, is only of use when you find you have some time on your hands and none of the above apply because you have not got any analytical skills whatsoever (not as unusual as you may think amongst the legal fraternity) or even the faintest inkling of any general knowledge. In these, let's hope rare, situations, there is one technique which may give you a little advantage.

It works on the assumption that few can tell before they answer a question just how well they are going to do in it, and just how good the answer itself is going to be. Thus, what you can do if you have about forty-five minutes left, one question still to do and you are hopelessly at sea, is to do *two*. You should plan to spend an imaginative twenty minutes on each, and then see how they have gone and cross out the worse of the two. If, after your twenty minutes on the first of these two alternatives, you have still not finished, then forget the plan and do that question properly as your fifth question.

One final thing. If you do adopt the technique above, do not lose count of the number of questions you have actually answered, and do not cross out the wrong answer by mistake.

POST-EXAMINATION

This does not apply to what you do once *all* the papers are over, because that is up to you and we all have different ways of dealing with that. This is more to do with once an individual paper is over, and the fact that you will still have other work to do before taking the next one.

I am definitely of the opinion that you should give yourself some time off before getting on with the revision that you need to do for the next paper. Of course, this is much easier if you have a day or two's gap before the next paper; it is a little harder to justify to yourself if you have just come out of an afternoon paper and you have a difficult one next morning.

However, your brain will slowly begin to cook at an increasingly high temperature if you pile straight into the next subject without at least a couple of hours relaxing. You will then get the increased benefit by working more efficiently for the next subject in the time available after your relaxing time. Go for a leisurely walk. Play a game of snooker if you must. Do anything you like. But take it easy for a while.

Of course this advice pre-supposes that you are a hard worker and not one of those people who needs no encouragement whatsoever to take time off. If you are one of those poor souls desperate for any excuse not to pick up the books and become once more embroiled in the intricacies of the *Cassis de Dijon* doctrine, then none of my above advice about relaxing applies. Get back to work you lazy, good-for-nothing waster! It is not over yet!

8
DOING IT IN STYLE

This is the chapter that will allow you to exercise a little more of your character than the dreadfully dull, boring and turgid (though of course absolutely essential) trawl through the notes and cases that you have been doing for so long. In a way it is something of a guide to one-up-manship of a peculiar type, namely within the sphere of study. There are those of you who, doubtless somewhat refined and superior, think that this is all a childish waste of time, and if so then I suggest that you skip this chapter entirely. Your loss if you do. For my part, I think that having fun is a serious business and some of these stratagems have given me hours of amusement.

Also, and this demonstrates the more unpleasant side of my character, I can think of fewer more enjoyable activities than playing on the inadequacies of my fellow students and ensuring that they realise (a) no matter how well prepared they are, they are still dull, and (b) the academic superiority that they feel by having been in the library since October is all an illusion. But then all life is an illusion, isn't it? Enough philosophy for the moment.

This campaign (the one-up-manship, not the philosophy) can be commenced at a much earlier stage than when your embryo academic ambitions caused you to open your first textbook at about Easter time. Take lectures, for example. I assume that, since you have decided to read this chapter, you are a relatively fun person to spend time with. The likelihood is therefore that you do not want to spend much time, if any, in lectures. I make no comment on the propriety or otherwise of this behaviour, but if you are going to miss lectures you may as well miss them properly!

For example, who is going to notice that you are not there if you never go in the first place? I recommend that everyone attends *all* their lectures for at least two weeks before contemplating missing any.

There are several reasons for this. The first is that there may be some lectures it is worth your while attending for the whole year. Unlikely, though, so let's move on. The next reason is that lectures are an excellent way of meeting other people. The third reason is that if you are to psyche out the others they have to know you exist in order for it to work satisfactorily. Then, after having struck up a couple of casual friendships, you can stop attending lectures and at least *someone* will notice.

The library is another excellent place to start emphasising your superiority. Of course, you must go to the library regularly (later on you will find out why) and learn where all the different sections are. However, you should not be seen reading law textbooks whilst in there. Far from it. If you must read them at all in November, read them at home in your room. No, you go to the library so that you can read the daily paper. Now, you have another choice. You can read the papers the library provides, and save yourself a little bit of cash each day, or you can buy your own. The latter course has its advantages. For example, if it is an exclusively law library, it may not have very interesting daily papers, and even if it does you will probably be required to read them in one particular area. You will therefore miss out on that excellent sport, reading your broadsheet in a loud rustling manner in a very crowded law library. I recommend that you indulge your weakness for this most enjoyable activity at least three or four times a week. It really is too much fun to miss out on. Oh, the happy times I have had covering my neighbours in the library with the arts pages of *The Independent*, or the sports pages of the *Daily Telegraph*! Excellent sport indeed. (I had to refer to both those papers so that you are not able to guess at my political allegiance.)

There are all sorts of other different ways to continue this sort of behaviour throughout the year. Some depend upon the topography of the particular town or city in which you are studying.

For example, where I went to college was a lovely little town in which there was a well travelled route to the lecture theatre along a pretty street.

Most students cycled, and those a little less unsightly walked, to lectures each morning. Fortuitously, this very street had a croissant shop – one might say a café – on that very same well-travelled route. The excellent thing about this café was that it had a very large front window, with delightful window tables. Hence one could sit there, sipping coffee and munching croissants, waving at all one's casual acquaintances (made in one's only two weeks of lecture attendance) as they passed on their way to another fun morning listening to the differences between fixtures and fittings.

This, however, was mere beginners' stuff compared to a story told me by a venerable chap who had been an undergraduate in the 1930s. He, as an engineer, was required to attend lectures every day, and cycled along that street each morning at about 8.55 am. Often, he would be hailed by a friend who would cross the street at about that time, in his slippers and dressing gown and carrying the morning paper, on the way to his bath (facilities being somewhat spartan in the 30s).

You may not be lucky enough to have such a conveniently placed café, or to have such a well-travelled route around which to plot your stratagem. If you live in London, say, it is highly unlikely that sitting in the window seat of a café and waving at passers-by will bring you anything more than the occasional physical assault when a passing builder mistakes your open friendliness. If you are in a big city, you may never even see your fellow students, because you all live in scattered and rather unpleasant quarters as the rent there is affordable as against absurd. (In some of these areas you may even find yourself actually paid to live there by a kind landlord, whom you later discover is running a crack house in the garden shed, masked by your apparent respectability.)

You will just have to organise your own campaign, to fit the spirit of one-up-manship into your circumstances. But never lose sight of the aim: do them down by living it up.

For this is what you should aspire to. The apparently effortless, yet effective, crushing of the spirit of those around you who concentrate too much on work and hence are no fun. They must be taught the errors of their ways, because that way some of them may see the light and reform whilst there is still time.

Thus all this should, if you aspire to real expertise, have been going on for some considerable period of time (as one particular politician, *not* an exponent of the genre, might say) by the arrival of the Easter rush. And this is the time that the *real* sport is to be had, during those weeks when the tension is increasing, the pressure building and the terror approaching. For everyone except you, that is. You should be wonderfully calm, relaxed and something of a joy to spend time with. You will be turning the screw, gently and imperceptibly, and chilling out in style.

HOLIDAYS

Such an important weapon in the arsenal for your campaign. If, whilst everyone else is stressed out and close to breaking point, you are not only too relaxed to get involved but actually go on holiday, you are way ahead of the game. And why not? Getting away from it all will do you the world of good.

A little time away from work, taking it easy, will not only be extremely good fun, but will help you to return refreshed and actually looking forward to doing some revision. But, in the same way as missing lectures, you have to go about it the right way, otherwise there is no point in doing it at all.

I shall tell you a little story now about a friend of mine. He was very talented when it came to taking life easy. I shall call him Fred – I have changed his name to save him from possible professional embarrassment now that he is a respected and upright member of a highly reputable law firm.

Fred had a particular technique that worked like a dream, but did depend on a little help. Don't be shy to enlist help in your schemes. You can either use a like-minded soul, in which case he or she will be only too pleased to help, or you can ask a nerd.

If the nerd behaves true to form, he or she will be amazed you have enlisted them and will help willingly. However, the nerd may refuse to help. If so, the very fact you have asked them will partly psyche them out and hence part of your goal has been achieved before you even reach the airport.

Fred's technique depended, as do most of the techniques, upon much hard work being put in behind the scenes beforehand. The reason for this is that there is not much point being cool and going on holiday if you then fail your exams. No one will be at all impressed – anyone can be a waster. You have to ensure that you do very well in your exams, because when the results come out you will put a little bit more mental pressure on them for next year's exams.

So, rather than trying to have a good holiday over the Easter vacation, attempting to forget how much work remained to be done once term started again, Fred would adopt the following pattern. He would work, hard, all through the three or four weeks of vacation. Of course, he had an incentive, because he knew he would get his holiday later.

So, while all his contemporaries worried, and attempted to get something of a break from it all (with a great deal on their minds), he would slave away, putting in the hours and compiling a vast amount of notes.

Then, at the beginning of term, all the other law students would arrive back at college dreading the coming weeks. Fred, on the other hand, would be just about to depart on his two-week break. Often, he would fly away to foreign climes. On his return, he would then have an amazing tan. Psyched out? You bet.

The help required (and provided by someone called Harry, who has also had his name changed for reasons of professional propriety) came about because of the peculiar rules of the particular establishment our two heroes attended. You see, there was a residency requirement which meant that, technically, Fred needed permission to go away in term-time. I do not know if Fred ever asked for permission, but I doubt it. After all, if he had asked and been refused then he would have had to disobey, wouldn't he? Far better not to ask at all. So Harry's role involved 'covering for' Fred whilst he was away. This took the form of, amongst other things (or inter alia, because I have to get some Latin in somewhere), pretending Fred was quite happily working away, making up references to conversations and meetings that never took place. Then, after about two weeks of this and just as the penny was about to drop as people were beginning to talk and realise that, in fact, the only one of their number who had supposedly seen Fred recently was his close buddy Harry, Fred would return from his hols. The amusing thing was he would, of course, have the aforesaid tan and everyone knew that something had been going on, but could not work out exactly what.

And then Fred and Harry would do an unusual thing. They would attend lectures for a day, having been absent from them since October. The reasons for this strange behaviour were numerous. One was to say hello to all the casual acquaintances they had neglected. Another was to demonstrate supreme lack of concern about what the lecturer was saying. Oh, and of course Fred had to show off his tan, and in reply to the question 'Where did you go at Easter?' could truthfully reply 'Nowhere, I was working,' thus scoring points. If the hapless questioner then continued 'So where did you get that tan?' Fred would, again completely truthfully, reply 'I have just returned from two weeks at Monte Carlo'. Yes, more points. What excellent sport.

There are variations on this technique, too, which you may like to try yourself. For example, Fred, as a canny Northern Celt concerned about cost, used to purchase very cheap airline tickets.

This had the effect of restricting the dates and times when he could depart, and prevented him from making the most of his departure. How much more fun it might have been, you may think, to have gone to lectures just before setting off and then again immediately upon return. How greater the 'before and after' contrast would have been.

Alternatively, and cost here is a factor which may prevent most of you, why go on holiday alone? You could ask a member of the opposite sex if they would care to join you on your little holiday. They will almost certainly say no, and you will have scored points because, of course, your secret is now out. Damn, I hate it when that happens. [Note: you must be aware that this plan could go wrong, and your invitation may be accepted. Depending upon who you have asked this could ruin your own well-deserved break and so issue such invitations only with the very greatest care.]

Of course, with the present level of student grants not everyone has the means whereby they can afford a holiday abroad. You do not need to. You can have a perfectly fun holiday in Skegness if you want. The only trouble with that is you are much more susceptible to the vagaries of the English climate if you stay at home. It may be more difficult to get a tan. You then have a choice – use a sunbed and pretend you have been away (not a bad idea but don't be found out) or go to Cornwall and, even if it does rain all the time, make sure that you spend all the time outside and at least you will end up looking weathered. Some may mistake it for a tan.

The next best thing, if you cannot manage a holiday for whatever reason, is simply to become a recluse. Absences can have the same effect, particularly if they are prolonged. Of course, and for reasons of personal safety, you should always make sure that someone knows exactly what is going on, but there is no reason why that person should be anything to do with your academic aspirations. A crucial part of this stratagem is to behave, on your occasional returns to the college environment, as if you have never been away. Thus, when you see your old colleagues, chat to them as if you saw them only yesterday.

If they fall into the trap and ask you 'Where have you been for the last six weeks?' you look at them blankly and say 'What do you mean? I have been here all the time.' The air of mystery will work wonders.

Which brings me to another of the stratagems. Disappear *completely* for the whole term. Just ensure that nobody whatsoever sees you at all, or knows where you are. You can then exercise one of the most rewarding plans of them all, the arrival at the first exam.

The reason that this particular one works so well is because people are, by virtue of human nature, extremely gossipy and full of rumour. Your absence will have caused the most bizarre rumours to have sprung up, and everyone will have a pet theory. Some will have you a nervous wreck, recovering at home or in an institution. Others will have the workload too much for you (try not to laugh) and you dropping out altogether. Then there will be those with a bit more faith in your diversity, who suggest that the government needed you for an important job in the Middle East and you had to drop everything and shoot off.

In reality you have been hiding, working away like a demon. Your arrival at the first exam must be planned carefully. You should not arrive so early that everyone can quiz you, but you must not get there so late that no one notices you arrive. You should appear calm, unruffled and relaxed, and your attire should reflect this. Something like a plain cotton suit, perhaps with a panama, suitably light in colour. Why? Because you have been toiling away stripped to the waist between two sun-lamps and you want to show off that tan. And then, to rub it in, you get a First.

IN CONTROL

Something you must always be, this means academically in control so that everyone knows it. In a way this is more difficult. You need to have done so much work that there is no doubt you *do* know it all, but you must be very careful so that you do not appear obnoxious. No one likes a smart alec, least of all me, and if you turn into one and blame it on this book I shall come around to your house with a transit van full of my friends wielding baseball bats. Enough of that.

But, for all the difficulties in the way of accomplishing this, it can reap its rewards. One of them is cross-reading. This is why I told you earlier to find your way around the library, so you know where *all* the different subjects are shelved. The reason for this is that you are a lawyer (or at least studying the subject) and everyone knows you are. Hence, ten days before the exams start you stride into the library purposefully and make your way, not to the law shelves, but to the medical book section. Try to do this in the middle of the afternoon when everyone is bored and will be attentive to your little tableau. If, by mischance, you happen to choose a time when a screamer is having his fit ten days early, quietly slip out and do it another day. (But just to pay the screamer back for wasting your journey all that way to the library, go up to him as the library staff are doing up the straps on the straitjacket and whisper 'You haven't got a hope, pal. You're going to fail for sure.' But perhaps you're not that vindictive.)

Back to the stratagem. All the people working in that section will probably be medics, and your arrival itself will create an air of interest. 'What is this lawyer doing in our neck of the woods?', they will ask themselves to begin with. Ignore everyone. You are a man or woman with a mission. Make your way directly to a shelf, and quickly select a book in such a way as though you know exactly what you are looking for. Briskly leaf through it, and stop at an appropriate passage which you quickly scan to discern a fact or two. All eyes will now be on you, believe me.

MEDICAL SECTION

C ⇨ F

You then triumphantly close the book with a slam, and choosing a youngster nearest to you (of the opposite sex if you are a flirt) say something like 'Hah! I *knew* the scaphoid had its own discrete blood supply. Haizheimer's new theory is absolute rubbish!' You then leave. (Of course you have made up the name Haizheimer, but they don't know that.)

If anyone is crass enough to say to you 'But you read law, don't you? What are you doing?' you give them a superior and slightly amused look. Try to be as patronising as you can. 'I'm reading around my subject, of course.' Then, added with an air of surprise, 'Don't you do that?' Who said you were allowed to psyche out only lawyers?

STUDY GROUPS

These are highly amusing developments from our transatlantic cousins. Apparently (and for reasons that will become apparent later I do not have first-hand knowledge of these things), people form groups (like therapy groups?) to study together. Why the blue blazes they do this I have not got the faintest idea. They have to take the exams themselves all on their own, so why they don't study the subject on their own I don't know.

Perhaps it is a symptom of people becoming unable (or not having the confidence) to do anything without involving someone else to hold their hand while they do it. You can gather, perhaps, that I have little time for this. But there is a further amusing chapter to my tirade against study groups.

I once took a post-graduate law degree. Quite a number of Americans were also on the course, as well as several Europeans. However, not the cool fun Americans that I have so much time for, or the excellent Europeans who live life and cook good food at the dinner parties I was eagerly anticipating they would hold, but nerds. Of course, each country has its fair share of nerds, and I do not suggest for a moment that there are more American nerds, or Euro-nerds, than any other nationality. But aren't embassies supposed to refuse these people visas? However, the upshot of these nerds' presence on the course included a bizarre style of dress; really not very cool – all chunky sweaters and stout boots.

I think someone had told them the weather in England was slightly worse than Scott encountered on his race to the South Pole. One student had even brought his huskies. They also had a burning and somewhat tedious desire to discuss serious issues. Why does anyone want to discuss serious issues at 10 o'clock in the morning? The most serious issue I have ever wanted to consider at that time is do I have a pain-au-chocolat or a croissant, and shall I have tea or coffee? Come to think of it, there are those who may say that I have never discussed a serious issue in my life, but certainly *never* with anyone I don't know very well. *Certainly* not a Euro-nerd.

In fact, the first time that I encountered this was in about October, whilst I was attending lectures and attempting to strike up some casual acquaintances. This cheery nerd came up to me and my friend and started chatting. No harm in that at all, of course, that was why I had attended the lecture in the first place. The only thing was, he started chatting about German philosophy. Was he trying to impress us? Was he just being a nerd? I don't know, but to begin with I mistook his blatherings for a very amusing bout of sarcasm and laughed heartily, expecting him to join in. He did not. He was not happy with me at all.

Needless to say, I was not invited to join a study group later in the year when they started revising 28 weeks before the exam. My friend, however, was. The assembled nerd committee, who convened to decide whom to invite to which study groups, decided to give him a chance denied me. I encouraged him to attend, obviously I did – I would have loved to go to one myself, just for fun – but he could not bear the thought of it. I am sadly unable to tell you what they do at these gatherings. If any of you get the chance, join one (just for a meeting or two) and write to me and tell me what happened. Oh, and try not to laugh at them. Nerds hate that.

Of course, you can always run your own study group. I suggest that you gather a collection of like-minded souls together, and choose one or two target nerds. Hold the first meeting and spend the whole hour or two discussing the 2.30 at Cheltenham, or the summer transfer market. The nerd will be utterly perplexed.

Alternatively, photocopy an old case that no one will have heard of, and that has nothing to do with any of your subjects. Start the meeting by asking if anyone knows the case; they will all say no. The nerd will sit there in the fond expectation that the next step is to read and discuss it. How wrong. When the last person has confessed that they, too, have never heard of the case, end the meeting (it should have lasted no more than ten minutes) by saying something like 'Well, that's that. Same time next week everyone?'

You should have the idea by now, I think. Endless hours of fun await you. The sport, the thrill of the stratagem, and then the delight when the thing works out will all give your summer a frisson that it would otherwise lack. Plus, and this is a bonus, the holiday will be fun in itself.

Of course, I expect you to refine your technique throughout your academic career. I had lunch at the Savoy just before the last exam I ever sat, which started at the very civilised time of 3 o'clock in the afternoon. As I remember, I cut it just a *little* bit too fine in that one, but what the heck? I psyched out most of my contemporaries, and that is all I was bothered about by then. None of that for you though, not yet anyway.

When the results come out and you realise that not only have you matched Cyril and Shirley but done far better than they have, you will know that I have been giving good sound advice. Because the plain fact of the matter is that it is not worth getting overheated about exams. My heart breaks when I hear tragic stories of students so worked up about these paltry tests that they do themselves physical or mental damage, or even worse. It is not that important. If you fail, think of all the entrepreneurs who dropped out of school and made a million before they were 25. You could do that. (If you do, take pity on me and send me a cheque.)

Alternatively, you could go to the Caribbean and open up a beach bar, or hire out deck-chairs. It could be quite a fun life.

But if you *do* pass, then you may very well need further guidance in your future professional life, in articles, pupillage or the like. There may be another book that could help you, and help to preserve the fun side of your life and stop you from becoming too work-oriented and, frankly, just plain dull. If there is such a book, it could be a powerful weapon in the right hands (ie yours).

You may suspect my motives, and ask why I should be recommending such a book. You may suspect that I, your guide thus far, may have written such a book myself, and am only encouraging you to buy it because I seek to establish my personal fortune.

You may very well think that. I could not possibly comment.

DETAILS FOR DESPATCH OF PUBLICATIONS

Please insert your full name below

Please insert below the style in which you would like the correspondence from the Publisher addressed to you
TITLE Mr, Miss etc.   INITIALS   SURNAME/FAMILY NAME

Address to which study material is to be sent (please ensure someone will be present to accept delivery of your Publications).

POSTAGE & PACKING
You are welcome to purchase study material from the Publisher at 200 Greyhound Road, London W14 9RY, during normal working hours.

If you wish to order by post this may be done direct from the Publisher. Postal charges are as follows:

UK   - Orders over £30: no charge. Orders below £30: £2.60. Single paper (last exam only): 55p
OVERSEAS   - See table below

The Publisher cannot accept responsibility in respect of postal delays or losses in the postal systems.

DESPATCH All cheques must be cleared before material is despatched.

SUMMARY OF ORDER

Date of order: _____

				£
			Cost of publications ordered:	
			UNITED KINGDOM:	

OVERSEAS:	TEXTS		Suggested Solutions (Last exam only)	
	One	Each Extra		
Eire	£5.00	£0.70	£1.00	
European Community	£10.50	£1.00	£1.00	
East Europe & North America	£12.50	£1.50	£1.50	
South East Asia	£12.00	£2.00	£1.50	
Australia/New Zealand	£14.00	£3.00	£1.70	
Other Countries (Africa, India etc)	£13.00	£3.00	£1.50	

Total cost of order: £ _____

Please ensure that you enclose a cheque or draft payable to **THE HLT GROUP LTD** for the above amount, or charge to ☐ Access ☐ Visa ☐ American Express

Card Number | | | | | | | | | | | | | | | | |

Expiry Date .... Signature ....

ORDER FORM

LLB PUBLICATIONS	TEXTBOOKS Cost £	£	CASEBOOKS Cost £	£	REVISION WORKBOOKS Cost £	£	SUG. SOL 1986/91 Cost £	£	SUG. SOL 1992 Cost £	£
Administrative Law	£18.95		£19.95				£9.95		£3.00	
Commercial Law Vol I	£18.95		£19.95		£9.95		£9.95		£3.00	
Commercial Law Vol II	£17.95		£19.95							
Company Law	£19.95		£19.95		£9.95		£9.95		£3.00	
Conflict of Laws	£18.95		£17.95		£9.95					
Constitutional Law	£16.95		£17.95		£9.95		£9.95		£3.00	
Contract Law	£16.95		£17.95		£9.95		£9.95		£3.00	
Conveyancing	£19.95		£17.95							
Criminal Law	£16.95		£18.95		£9.95		£9.95		£3.00	
Criminology	£17.95						£4.95†		£3.00	
English Legal System	£16.95		£14.95		£9.95		£8.95*		£3.00	
European Community Law	£17.95		£19.95		£9.95		£4.95†		£3.00	
Equity and Trusts	£16.95		£17.95		£9.95					
Evidence	£19.95		£18.95		£9.95		£9.95		£3.00	
Family Law	£18.95		£19.95		£9.95		£9.95		£3.00	
Jurisprudence	£16.95				£9.95		£9.95		£3.00	
Land Law	£16.95		£17.95		£9.95		£9.95		£3.00	
Law of Trusts							£9.95		£3.00	
Public International Law	£18.95		£18.95		£9.95		£9.95		£3.00	
Revenue Law	£19.95		£19.95		£9.95		£9.95		£3.00	
Roman Law	£14.95									
Succession	£19.95		£18.95		£9.95		£9.95		£3.00	
Tort	£16.95		£17.95		£9.95		£9.95		£3.00	

BAR PUBLICATIONS

	TEXTBOOKS Cost £	£	CASEBOOKS Cost £	£	REVISION WORKBOOKS Cost £	£	SUG. SOL 1986/91 Cost £	£	SUG. SOL 1992 Cost £	£
Conflict of Laws	£18.95		£17.95				£9.95§		£4.50	
Civil & Criminal Procedure	£21.95		£20.95				£14.95		£4.50	
European Community Law & Human Rights	£17.95		£19.95				£9.95§		£4.50	
Evidence	£19.95		£18.95				£14.95		£4.50	
Family Law	£18.95		£19.95				£14.95		£4.50	
General Paper I	£21.95		£20.95				£14.95		£4.50	
General Paper II	£21.95		£20.95				£14.95		£4.50	
Law of International Trade	£17.95		£19.95				£14.95		£4.50	
Practical Conveyancing	£19.95		£17.95				£14.95		£4.50	
Revenue Law	£19.95		£19.95				£14.95		£4.50	
Sale of Goods & Credit	£18.95		£18.95				£14.95		£4.50	

* 1987–1991
† 1990–1991
§ 1988–1991

HLT PUBLICATIONS

All HLT Publications have two important qualities. First, they are written by specialists, all of whom have direct practical experience of teaching the syllabus. Second, all Textbooks are reviewed and updated each year to reflect new developments and changing trends. They are used widely by students at polytechnics and colleges throughout the United Kingdom and overseas.

A comprehensive range of titles is covered by the following classifications.

- **TEXTBOOKS**
- **CASEBOOKS**
- **SUGGESTED SOLUTIONS**
- **REVISION WORKBOOKS**

The books listed above should be available from your local bookshop. In case of difficulty, however, they can be obtained direct from the publisher using this order form. Telephone, Fax or Telex orders will also be accepted. Quote your Access, Visa or American Express card numbers for priority orders. To order direct from publisher please enter cost of titles you require, fill in despatch details overleaf and send it with your remittance to The HLT Group Ltd.